Islam: A Primer

Revised Edition

John Sabini

Middle East Editorial Associates
Washington, District of Columbia

Arabic Calligraphy: Mohamed Zakariya

Cover Design and Maps: Paddy McLoughlin, Concepts & Design

LIBRARY OF CONGRESS CATALOGING-IN-PUBLICATION DATA
Sabini, John, 1921–
    Islam, a primer / John Sabini. —Rev. ed.
        p. cm.
    Includes bibliographical references.
    ISBN 0-918992-08-7
    1. Islam.   I. Title
BP161.2.S18   1994   90-62397
297—dc20   CIP

Published in the United States of America by
Middle East Editorial Associates
1730 M Street, N.W., Suite 100
Washington, D.C. 20036-4045

PREFACE

This introduction to Islam is designed for the reader who is not familiar with Islam and would like to acquire a general knowledge of its origins and beliefs. As both a faith and a civilization, Islam has existed for fourteen centuries and embraces a fifth of the world's population; a concise account such as this, therefore, can deal only with the highlights. A suggested reading list is provided at the end of the book for those who wish to learn more.

In a primer about Islam it is not possible to describe in detail how the practice of Islam varies from country to country, and the author, after offering an encompassing introduction to the Muslim world in the first chapter, leaves to others the task of interpreting the turbulent politics of the contemporary Middle East. In this context, readers should note that current Muslim extremist movements, though highly vocal and often in the public eye, represent but a small segment of the Islamic mainstream.

It is hoped that the background provided in this survey will provide insight into the true character and direction of modern Islamic society.

TABLE OF CONTENTS

KEY TERMS AND NAMES

In order to understand Islam it is necessary to know the meaning of certain key terms and the identity of some proper names. Most of them are in the Arabic language, and there is often no equivalent in English or in other European tongues. As this book is meant to be read in whatever order the reader may find useful, it would be cumbersome and repetitious to define these terms or identify the names each time they appear. Therefore, they are listed immediately below. Other terms and names which are useful in understanding particular aspects of Islam are listed in the glossary at the back of the book.

Islam means submission, that is, submission to the will of God, the characteristic attitude of members of the Islamic faith.

Muslim (also spelled Moslem) is based on the same Arabic root as Islam (s-l-m) and means one who submits to God, that is, a believer in Islam. It is incorrect and objectionable to call members of this religion Muhammadans, as they do not worship Muhammad in the way that Christians worship Christ.

Allah is the Supreme Being, the one and only God. According to Islam Allah is the same God as that worshipped by the Jews and Christians, and Arabic-speaking Christians also use this name when referring to God.

Muhammad is the prophet or apostle of God. He was born in Arabia about 570 and died in 632. According to Islam he was the last of a line of prophets, including many of those of the Old Testament and Jesus Christ.

The *Quran* (also spelled Koran, Coran, Alkoran, etc.) is the holy scripture of Islam revealed by Allah to Muhammad. The word Quran means readings or recitations.

Mecca (also spelled Makkah) is the caravan town where Muhammad was born and raised. It is near the west coast of Arabia about 45 miles (72 kilometers) from the seaport of Jiddah and about midway between the northern and southern ends of the Red Sea.

Medina (also spelled Madina) is another caravan town about 280 miles (447 kilometers) north of Mecca, where Muhammad spent the last ten years of his life and where he is buried. Originally called Yathrib, it became known as *Madinat al-Nabi,* City of the Prophet, and hence Medina.

Ka'ba, meaning "cube" in Arabic, is the principal shrine of Islam, located in Mecca. It is the center of the Muslim pilgrimage and the point towards which all Muslims the world over face in prayer.

Sunna means "tradition" and is the sum of the sayings and actions of Muhammad as recalled by his companions and followers. As such it is second only to the Quran as a source of Islamic belief and practices. Sunna (adjective Sunni or Sunnite) also denotes the mainstream or "orthodox" body of Muslims as opposed to Shi'a.

Shi'a (adjective Shi'i or Shi'ite) is the minority division (10-15 percent) of Islam, consisting of scores of dissident sects opposed to Sunna Islam and to one another. The name means "party" in the political sense and comes from *Shi'at Ali,* the party of Ali.

Ali was a cousin of Muhammad and married to the Prophet's daughter Fatima. He was elected fourth caliph of Islam but lost his position through warfare and arbitration. The resulting conflict split Islam into the sects that exist today. His followers are called *Alids.*

Hadith, meaning communication or narrative, is the record of an individual saying or action of Muhammad taken as a model of behavior by Muslims.

Caliph, from Arabic *khalifa,*means deputy or successor and is the title of the theoretical leader of Islam. The caliphate is now vacant in Sunni Islam. The Shi'ite sects have complicated beliefs concerning it.

All quotations from the Quran are taken from *The Glorious Kur'an,* translation and commentary by Abdallah Yousef Ali.

All dates are Anno Domini unless otherwise indicated.

A note on transliteration—The transfer of Arabic words into the Roman characters of the English language, a near hopeless task at best, may not always meet the approval of the experts. The main concern has been to enable the reader to travel through the text without unduly tripping over unfamiliar markings and letter combinations.

1

THE WORLD OF ISLAM

Islam is one of the major religions of the world, embracing an estimated one-fifth of the total world population. Originating in Arabia in the seventh century, it spread rapidly across a broad geographical stretch of the globe—from the Atlantic coast of Africa in the west to the fringes of the Pacific in the east, and from equatorial Africa in the south to the steppes of central Asia in the north. In the course of this expansion, it assimilated many different peoples, as diverse as the Persians, the Berbers of North Africa, the Turks and Mongols of western Asia, and a large proportion of the people of India, Africa and southeastern Europe. With few exceptions, it has retained the loyalty of these peoples, who now make up the Islamic nations of today. It is still growing in numbers and expanding geographically through conversion, immigration and high birth rates.

The Prophet of Islam, Muhammad, was not only a great religious teacher but also a military and political leader of genius. Islam's holy book, the Quran, to a Muslim the word of God, is a work of high moral principles, spiritual vision and far-reaching social reform. Its all-embracing concept of

1

unity and faith in one God has persuaded generations of its truth and satisfied their highest spiritual aspirations.

Islam is a way of life as well as a religion. The Quran and the teachings of Muhammad contain precise and detailed legal and social prescriptions that govern every aspect of life for the believer. As a result Islam transformed the societies in which it became dominant. In the process it created a brilliant civilization which flourished in different parts of the world for more than a thousand years. Islamic culture at its height was far superior to that of western Europe and many of its contributions were vital to the European Renaissance.

During the 20th century, there has been a remarkable revitalization in the Islamic world after several hundred years of subordination to Western power and influence. As a result of these influences, the Muslim people have been undergoing transitional change on many levels in their lives. The religion of Islam, however, continues to retain an extraordinary hold over its members, a hold that is stronger and broader than that of Christianity over its adherents. Christianity, unlike Islam, has passed through a number of historical experiences—the Renaissance, the Reformation, the Age of Reason, the scientific revolution, and the appearance of secular philosophies such as Utilitarianism, logical positivism and Marxism. Consequently, Christianity has lost importance as the foundation of thought and action in most spheres of human endeavor. In politics, for example, this can be summed up in the doctrine of the separation of church and state, an idea alien to Islam.

Islam has undergone none of these changes, except as

[handwritten marginal note: is Christianity is seriously strong? No, like freeing.]

echoes from the West. In this century, however, all Muslim societies have been facing a wave of dramatic change, and this has brought with it a sense of insecurity and apprehension. Deeply concerned by the threat of secularization and the disintegration of their religious and cultural heritage, Muslims cling to an Islamic base of identity despite their desire for the benefits offered by modern technology.

The current Islamic revival, most evident and active in Iran but also reverberating to varying degrees in other Muslim countries, is in essence a reaction against the West and the cultural consequences of adopting its path of modernization. The material benefits of technology have reached only a small minority of people in some countries and this has dramatically widened the socioeconomic gap; more than ever, the Islamic masses feel their poverty and are readily aroused by any promise of reform. Many of the young and unemployed, suffering economic impotence and cultural disorientation, have turned to the traditional values of Islam for an answer. They seek to establish the ethically based social order which they believe in as a principle of Islam—the concept of communal sharing and solidarity upon which the faith was founded fourteen centuries ago.

The sociopolitical manifestation of Islamic revivalism cannot be separated from the religion itself, since Islam in practice penetrates and influences all aspects of a Muslim's life. Political action in the Muslim world is often linked to the power and influence of a religious leader. In some countries the return to Islamic traditions has been violent and extreme, but even more moderate Muslims are seeking an increasingly Islamic stance—i.e., non-Western and non-secular—in their private and public lives.

Therefore, in order to understand the individual and collective behavior of Muslims today, it is necessary to know something about their religion as well as the culture and civilization Islam produced. On the simplest level, for example, it is impossible to understand Muslims without some knowledge of the Quranic conception of faith, law and society. On the national level of government, although many Islamic states are authoritarian in form, it is important to note a democratic tendency based on the Quranic doctrine of consensus among the qualified members of the community. On an international level, the unity of Islam is still a potent ideal, despite the frequent dissension among individual states. The ancient divisions within Islam, such as those between the Sunna and the various branches of the Shi'a, are reflected in political differences within communities and between states. Muslim attitudes toward capitalism and communism, and toward such diverse matters as marriage, birth control, education, and crime and punishment are mostly based on Quranic principles or precedents.

The sheer numbers of Muslims and their distribution make their ideas and attitudes important to the rest of the world. The total number of Muslims today is estimated at more than a billion. Muslims form nearly the total population (90 percent or more) in approximately twenty-five countries and a majority (50 percent or more) in another ten. Among the states dominated by Muslim majorities are all the countries of the Arabian Peninsula, plus Morocco, Algeria, Tunisia, Libya, Egypt, Sudan, Afghanistan, Turkey, Syria, Lebanon, Jordan, Iran, Iraq, Pakistan, Bangladesh, Malaysia and Indonesia. There are large Muslim minorities in other countries, including 88 million in India, 53 million in the U.S.S.R., 35 million in Nigeria, 16 million in China, 5.6 million in South Africa, 2.6 million in Yugoslavia, as well as 1 million in Britain and 4 million in the United States.

As can be seen, the largest concentrations of Muslims are found in the Third World among the emerging nations, with all that this implies for restlessness and change. The economic potential of the Muslim world is indicated by the fact that 70 percent of the world's oil reserves lies in Muslim states: estimated reserves, in barrels, of 255 billion in Saudi Arabia, 100 billion in Iraq, 98 billion in United Arab Emirates, 95 billion in Kuwait, 93 billion in Iran, 22 billion in Libya, 17 billion in Nigeria, 8 billion each in Algeria and Indonesia.

*The inherent power of Islam to affect the world we live in is perhaps the most important reason for us to know something about the origin, beliefs and practices of Islam.

2

BASIC BELIEFS

In essence, there are many similarities between the beliefs of Islam and those of Judaism and Christianity. This is not surprising, as Muhammad is in the tradition of Moses and Jesus in conveying the word of God. His aim was not to found a new religion but to correct and complete the message of his predecessors.

Principles and Tenets

Six principles define the beliefs of Islam. They relate to the supremacy of God, Muhammad as the messenger of God, the Quran as the word of God, the immortal existence of angels (and the devil as a fallen angel), sin and the final judgment.

The fundamental belief is the absolute oneness of God. This is proclaimed again and again in the Quran, most clearly in the verse:

> Say, He is God the One and Only,
> God the Eternal, the Absolute:
> He begetteth not nor is He begotten,
> And there is none like unto Him. (Sura CXII)

The corollary of this is that any association of another

being with God is the unforgivable sin of *shirk* (association or polytheism), thus ruling out any veneration of minor gods, idols, human saints, or a divine consort or son. Even Muhammad, though the greatest of prophets, is merely a man, not to be worshipped or called upon to intercede between man and God.

Next to this uncompromising monotheism, the most important doctrine in Islam is that God has revealed his divine will through the Prophet Muhammad and that the holy book of the Quran is the completion of this revelation. God is transcendent—that is, prior to and apart from the created universe—and beyond all comparison. But he is a personal God, "as near as the vein in one's neck," and can therefore be approached directly without an intermediary such as a priest or a saint. God's power and knowledge are infinite. He is merciful and compassionate and hates oppression and injustice. He requires from mankind submission, truthfulness and trust. On the Day of Judgment, every person's sins and good deeds will be weighed in a balance, and God will send whom he wills to a paradise of delights or a hell of torment.

Heaven and Hell. Islam believes strongly in an afterlife, in which human beings are rewarded or punished according to their conduct on earth. Judgment, however, is postponed until the Last Day. In the meantime the soul remains in the grave, where it receives a foretaste of its fate.

The Quran contains two versions of Paradise. One is a garden flowing with rivers of sweet water, milk, wine and honey and planted with fruit and shade trees. In later verses the Quran presents a more austere version of Paradise. It is a pyramid or cone of eight levels, its top shaded by a lotus tree, its walls guarded by angels. The elect are lodged in rising order according to their merit. The prototypes of the Quran and the Ka'ba are kept in Paradise, and so are the records of men's deeds to be weighed on Judgment Day, and the standard of the Prophet. Paradise is located above the visible heavens and rests on a number of seas. Above it is the throne of God.

The two versions of Paradise are not necessarily contradictory, although the tone of each is different. The later version obviously inspired Dante's description in *The Divine Comedy*. The 11th-century Muslim theologian al-Ghazali believed that the pleasures of Paradise were more imaginary than sensual and included the joys of the intellect. He thought that the greatest reward of the elect was the presence of God.

Hell in the Quran is generally conceived of as a place—called *jahannam* (related to the Hebrew *gehenna*). Sometimes it seems to be a person, as when God says, "Bring Hell" on the Last Day and "Hell shall burst with fury." Hell is a reverse image of Paradise, a crater of seven concentric rings or terraces, one less than in Paradise, as fewer souls will be consigned to Hell. Each ring has a gate, and punishments are graded downward according to the severity of the sin. A bridge as narrow as the edge of a sword spans the mouth of Hell; the souls of the righteous will cross it with more or less ease, while those of the wicked will fall into the crater. Al-Ghazali says that the bridge is simply the life of man on earth.

Angels, Jinns and Devils. The Quran speaks of three classes of creatures other than mankind—angels, jinns and devils. Angels (*malaika*) are the messengers and slaves of God. They were formed of light, but appear in various guises and are commanded by four archangels, Jibril (Gabriel), Mikail, Izrail and Israfil.

A belief in jinns was common in pre-Islamic Arabia, where they probably represented the old animistic gods. The Quran retained them as a separate creation, and Muhammad preached to them as well as to men and women. Jinns are created of fire; they are intelligent, physically strong, usually imperceptible yet capable of appearing in various forms. In folklore they are connected with magic and talismans and can be made to serve men. Some Muslim philosophers, however, doubted their existence; Ibn Khaldoun, one of the greatest of Muslim thinkers, said the truth about them was known only to Allah.

Devils in Islam are associated with jinns, although they are of a different class of beings. The Quran speaks of *shaitan* (Satan) in the singular and also in the plural (*shayatiyn*). Devils do not reside in Hell but will be sent there at the end of time. One of their weapons against mankind is disease, especially the plague. In religious thought, Shaitan is the power in man's heart that is opposed to God.

The Holy Quran

Muslims believe that the Quran is a transcript of parts of a book that is preserved in Heaven and in which all that has ever happened and all that ever will happen is recorded.

> This is the Book;
> In it is guidance sure, without doubt,
> To those who fear God. (Sura II)

The Quran is literally the Word of God. It contains the will of God as revealed in the Arabic language for all Muslims. The Jewish Torah and the Christian Gospel also contain the will of God as revealed to those people; Muslims believe that the Quran completes the revelation and restores it to the pristine truth. It is infallible and immutable.

The text of the Quran was transmitted to Muhammad piecemeal over a period of twenty-two years by a Holy Spirit, traditionally identified as the angel Gabriel. Muhammad was in a state of spiritual communion when the messages that comprise the Quran were revealed to him. His remarks, observations and actions—made in a normal state and second in importance to the Quran—are recorded in the Hadith, the traditions of the Prophet. He delivered the Quranic revelations orally to his followers who committed them to memory. On his instructions some of the messages were recorded during his lifetime, often in a haphazard manner, on palm leaves, flat stones, the shoulder blades of camels or scraps of parchment. The Quran was finally compiled in its present form in 651, nineteen years after the Prophet's death.

Form. The Quran is divided into 114 chapters (*sura*), and the chapters divided into verses (*aya*), numbering 6,236 in all. The chapters vary in length from 3 to 282 ayas. Scholars can distinguish between the revelations at Mecca and those at Medina, which are known as the earlier and later suras. The Meccan suras tend to be short and deal with religious themes, while the Medinan suras are usually longer and deal with specific legal, social or political situations and can only be understood with knowledge of the circumstances in which they were revealed.

Muslims believe that the meaning of the Quran is inseparable from the language in which it was revealed. Although there are interpretations of the Quran in other languages, the true Quran is in Arabic. Therefore Muslims everywhere, whatever their native tongue, recite the Quran only in its Arabic original.

All students of Arabic, whether Muslim or not, agree that the Quran is incomparable. It is extraordinarily concise yet rich in its imagery, with a rhythm and cadence of peculiar beauty. Many of the suras are written in plain prose, but the majority are in rhymed verse. The syntax is often complex, even to educated Arabs, and some of the words used appear nowhere else in Arabic literature.

Content. An unbiased reading of the Quran reveals it to be one of the great religious books of the world. It sets forth the theological and moral basis of a faith that has satisfied the religious aspirations and exalted the spirits of a large part of mankind for the past fourteen centuries. It contains a rich storehouse of legends, stories common to the Bible, moral maxims, ecstatic verse and legal precepts. It reveals a noble concept of deity and of man's moral obligations. It treats of eternal themes in an original and powerful manner.

Even in translation the devotional poetry is of a very high order:

> God is the light
> Of the heavens and the earth.
> The parable of His Light
> Is as if there were a Niche
> And within it a Lamp,
> The Lamp enclosed in Glass:
> The glass as it were
> A brilliant star:
> Lit from a blessed Tree,
> An olive, neither of the East
> nor of the West,
> Whose Oil is well-nigh luminous
> Though fire scarce touched it:
> Light upon Light!
> God doth guide
> Whom He will
> To His light. (Sura XXIV)

Muslims venerate the Quran with an intensity hardly known to Jews or Christians. Some learn the entire book by heart; all can recite large parts of it. It provides quotations for every occasion, both public and private, and consolation in all circumstances. Some people never leave home without a copy. It must be treated with great respect: no other book is allowed to be placed over it; it should be carried above the waist; one must not smoke or drink while reading it or listening to it. It is a talisman against disease or disaster. Quranic inscriptions are chiseled in stone, painted on tiles or woven in cloth for public and private use. Copies of the Quran have been illuminated and embellished to create great works of Islamic art. Because of its association with the Quran, Arabic calligraphy developed into one of the fine arts.

As Muhammad often said to his detractors, the Quran itself was his only miracle and proved him to be among the prophets.

Sunna: The Traditions of The Prophet

In addition to the Quran—the holy word of God—Islam is based on the traditions of the Prophet, that is the sayings and actions of Muhammad as recalled and transmitted by his contemporaries. These traditions, called collectively the *sunna* of the Prophet, are of almost equal weight as the revelations of divine will given in the Quran, and in many cases they interpret and define the often cryptic passages in the Holy Book. Sunna is also the name of the major branch of Islam, whose followers are called Sunnites (or Sunni), and who comprise 85 to 90 percent of the Muslim people.

The Hadith. In the years immediately following the death of Muhammad, the Muslims had only to turn to those closest to him in life—his widow Aisha was a rich source—to determine what the Prophet did or said on a particular occasion or what his reply was to a question concerning the right or wrong way of thinking or acting. As time went on and Muhammad's contemporaries died off, it became necessary to collect the traditions and to record them for the use of judges and others in authority, as well as for ordinary people. The record of an individual tradition was called a *hadith*, meaning "communication" or "narrative." Each hadith had to be supported by a chain of authorities going back to Muhammad. Thus a hadith consisted of two parts: the chain of authorities (A said that B said that C said ...that the Prophet told him or did on such and such an occasion) followed by the substance of the hadith.

As the Muslims conquered new territories and began to split into factions, an enormous number of hadiths came into circulation, many of them contradictory and plainly not in accordance with relevant passages in the Quran. Hadiths were introduced supporting rival claimants to the caliphate, or authorizing practices and beliefs native to the new territories and congenial to new converts. Shi'ite Islam, for example, accepted only hadiths stemming from its founder Ali and his partisans. By the 10th century the Abbasid caliphs, who then ruled the Muslim world, ordered a critical examination and reform of tradition, which reduced the number of hadiths in circulation from some 600,000 to about 3,000. The method of elimination was to establish the authenticity of the chain of authorities and also to examine the credibility of the substance of each hadith. This led to the writing of the first biographies of the leaders of early Islam, with an eye to their degree of intimacy with the Prophet and of the likelihood of their familiarity to others in the chain of authority. By this method hadiths were divided into three categories: the genuine, the good and the weak. A certain amount of inconsistency remained and is tolerated by the most orthodox Muslims. Between Sunni and Shi'ites, however, there is wide disagreement on which hadiths are acceptable.

Many of the hadiths deal with abstruse points of the Law (*Shari'a*) or with religious dogma and the minutiae of religious practice. The rituals of prayer and of pilgrimage, for example, are almost entirely based on tradition. Some hadiths allude to particular events and situations during the career of the Prophet which must be known before they can be interpreted. Some reinforce statements already made clear and complete in the Quran, while others extend

or modify Quranic injunctions. "Wine is the
is a hadith reinforcing the Quranic ban
drink. Although the Quran specifically perm
hadith sheds an entirely different light on
stating "of lawful things the most hateful to Go   ...ce."
There are hadiths prohibiting suicide and condemning
murderers to eternal damnation. Others show the importance that Muhammad attached to matters of personal
hygiene, as well as proper table manners. Many hadiths
deal with women. "The true veil is in the eyes of men"
poses a nice question as to where modesty and immodesty
lie. "Of worldly things, women and perfume are made dear
to me and the comfort of my eyes is made in prayer" gives
an intimate glimpse into the private life of Muhammad. It
seems that no subject is too large or too small to be
covered by a hadith.

The Five Pillars of Islam

Among the specific duties set forth in the Quran and
spelled out in the traditions are the Five Pillars of Islam.
These are five specific actions which a Muslim must perform in order to be on the right path. They are testimony to
faith, prayer, almsgiving, fasting and the pilgrimage.

The First Pillar: testimony (shahada). This is the
profession of faith: "There is no god but God; Muhammad
is the messenger of God." The statement contains the essence of Islam: the unity and uniqueness of God and the
role of Muhammad in bringing the message of God to
mankind. In its melodious Arabic form, "La ilaha illa Allah;
Muhammad rasul Allah," it is repeated every day by all

devout Muslims throughout the world and is heard in the *muezzin's* call of the faithful to prayer. It is also seen in inscriptions on buildings and on the coins and flags of some Muslim states.

The Second Pillar: prayer (*salah*). This is not simply by personal choice in time or manner but in the form of ritualized worship. The Quran promises that those who pray and perform good deeds will enter Paradise, and tradition states that each salah absolves one of minor sins. The Quran calls on all Muslims to pray regularly and at frequent intervals; the form and timing of the salah have been fixed by tradition. Every adult Muslim, male or female, of sound mind and body, is required to pray five times a day—at sunset (the beginning of the Muslim day), in the evening, at dawn, at noon and in mid-afternoon. The hours are announced by the call of the muezzin from the mosque (now often transmitted by radio or television). Salah may be performed in private, but it is better if done in the company of others and preferably in a mosque. When praying communally, the worshippers form in lines behind a chosen leader, called an *imam* and face in the direction of the *Ka'ba* in Mecca. The worshipper must be in a state of ritual purity, accomplished by washing the face and the hands and arms up to the elbow, rubbing water on the head, and washing or rubbing the feet. A fountain is provided for this purpose in the mosque, but if no water is available, clean sand may be used instead. The worshipper removes his shoes or sandals and stands on a special rug or mat to maintain cleanliness. Women for reasons of modesty do not usually perform salah in public. If they must do so (when traveling, for instance), they stand behind the men in a separate row.

Above all, salah should be performed devoutly, with solemnity and decorum, but without undue emotion or false humility. A Muslim at prayer should not be interrupted, stared at, photographed or passed in front of. Salah must be performed in Arabic, whatever the language of the worshipper. The ritual of salah follows a set form throughout the world, though variations of length and Quranic texts are permitted. The worshipper bows several times while repeating devotional phrases, such as *Allahu akbar* (God is most great) and recites the opening verse of the Quran:

> Praise be to God,
> The Cherisher and Sustainer of the Worlds;
> Most Gracious, Most Merciful;
> Master of the Day of Judgment.
> Thee do we worship,
> And Thine aid we seek. (Sura I)

He may recite other verses, and he kneels and prostrates himself with hands and face on the ground. At the end he rises and pronounces the testimony of faith and, looking round him, says to his companions, "Peace be upon you and the mercy of God."

Besides the five daily salahs, Muslims perform other prayers for special occasions. The midday salah on Friday, which is the Muslim sabbath, is communal and every able-bodied man is expected to go to the mosque. Special salahs are held on the great feast days of Islam. Salahs are also said for the dead, to induce rain during drought or to avert a calamity that threatens the community.

As with other major religions, prayer in Islam is both an

act of personal devotion and a communal rite reinforcing the unity of the faithful.

The Third Pillar: payment of the alms tax (*zakah*). Charity is one of the principal duties imposed by the Quran, and benevolence towards the less fortunate is highly praised. In theory almsgiving is divided into the obligatory (*zakah*) and the voluntary (*sadaqa*) but the distinction is not always maintained. The zakah prescribes a system of fixed taxes in money or kind on the possessions of Muslims. In early times zakah was collected by the state, and this is still the case in traditional Muslim states, where it takes the place of income tax. Elsewhere Muslims voluntarily make the collection among themselves and dispense it for the welfare of the community, primarily to help the poor. In addition Muslims are by tradition openhanded to street beggars. On feast days they give generously to the poor and bestow alms to atone for any involuntary breaking of a fast.

The Fourth Pillar: fasting (*sawm*). Once a year for a period of one month Muslims are required to abstain from food, drink, smoking and sexual relations during the hours of daylight. This occurs during Ramadan, the ninth month of the Islamic calendar, when Muhammad received the first revelation. As the Islamic year is lunar and thus is ten to eleven days shorter than the solar year, the months move gradually through the seasons. The fast is difficult enough during the short cool days of winter; in summer it can be a severe hardship.

The fast is meant to test the self-denial and submission of the faithful and permit the rich to experience the deprivations of the poor. Both men and women and all but the youngest children keep the fast. The sick, pregnant women and those on long journeys may delay fasting until a more convenient time or, if unable to fast, pay alms for each day the fast is broken. In some Muslim countries the day-long fast is enforced by law. All restaurants are closed, hours of food shops restricted and smoking in public is prohibited. Non-Muslims are expected to refrain from any provocative display of their exemption from the fast. Muslims are urged to give generously to charity during Ramadan. The *zakah al-fitr* donation is a day's supply of food from each family member.

Paradoxically, Ramadan can be one of the merriest seasons of the Muslim year in some countries. In the evening special foods are served to break the fast and families and friends feast into the night. Many people take to the streets for communal festivities. The mosques are brightly lit and filled with worshippers. Parts of the towns are turned into fairgrounds; shops, cafes and places of amusement are open; children, allowed to stay up late, ride on swings and merry-go-rounds. Most people get little sleep, as an hour or so before dawn men march through the streets beating drums to awaken everyone for a final meal before the day's fasting begins. As the month draws to a close, everyone scans the sky for the appearance of the new moon marking the end of the fast. News of the sighting is traditionally conveyed by the booming of a cannon (now more usually by radio and television). This is the signal for the start of *Id al-Fitr,* literally the Feast of Breaking the Fast, which lasts for three days or more. Children receive presents, new clothes are worn, and alms given to the poor.

The Fifth Pillar: pilgrimage (*hajj*). The Quran requires that every adult Muslim of either sex and in sound body and mind make a pilgrimage to Mecca at least once in a lifetime if possible. Exemptions are permitted for the sick, the insane, and women who have no husbands or other male relatives to accompany them.

Pilgrimage is of two kinds. *Umrah,* the lesser pilgrimage, may be made at any time of the year and is voluntary. *Hajj,* the required pilgrimage, must be made during the twelfth month, *Dhu al-Hijjah.* Despite the difficulties and expense of traveling from distant places to Mecca, most Muslims perform the Hajj with enthusiasm, not only for its religious meaning, but as an opportunity to travel, to see the historical sites of Islam and to meet and mingle with Muslims from other parts of the world. Anyone who makes the pilgrimage is entitled to be called *hajji* and is held in great respect thereafter.

Muslims believe that the rites of the pilgrimage were taught to Adam by the archangel Gabriel and that Abraham (Ibrahim), the ancestor of both the Jews and the Arabs, also performed them. With time, however, the shrine in Mecca and the ceremonies became polluted by polytheism, and it was Muhammad's mission to restore the people to the worship of Allah, the one true God. Although the Quran does not describe the rituals of the prayer, the rites performed today are based on the tradition of those performed by Muhammad during his last pilgrimage.

The pilgrim must enter the holy territory that surrounds Mecca in a state of ritual purity. Having bathed and trimmed his hair, beard and nails, the male pilgrim dons the *ihram*—two sheets of seamless white cloth, one wrapped around the hips, the other draped over the shoulders. He must not cover his head or feet, though he may wear sandals and carry a sunshade. Women wear a simple white robe and a veil that covers the head but not the face. This uniformity of dress is meant to remove all distinctions of class, wealth and origin among the pilgrims. Throughout the Hajj, pilgrims may not cut their hair, trim their nails, wear jewelry or perfume, or indulge in sexual intercourse. Each group of pilgrims is led through the rites of worship by a hajj-guide who speaks the language of the group.

The destination of every pilgrim is the Holy Mosque in Mecca that contains the Ka'ba. The Ka'ba is a nearly cubical structure of dark stone about fifty feet high, which Muslims believe was built by Ibrahim and his son Ismail. It stands in a large courtyard containing several smaller structures and a colonnade. The pilgrim circles the Ka'ba seven times (*the tawaf*), trying at least once to touch or to kiss the sacred Black Stone, which is embedded in a corner of the building. Believed to have been sent down from Heaven by God in ancient times, the Black Stone is about twelve inches across, black with a reddish hue and surrounded by a silver collar. Over the centuries the touch of countless pilgrims has worn it smooth. After kissing or touching the Black Stone, the pilgrim then runs several times between two hills near the Ka'ba and drinks from the holy well of Zamzam. These actions are said to commemorate Hagar's search for water in the desert for herself and her son Ismail. The pilgrims pray and recite passages from the Quran during these rites and may hear a sermon preached by the imam of the Mosque. The rites described so far are part of the umrah as well as of the Hajj proper.

On the eighth day of the month of the Hajj the pilgrims pour out of Mecca through a mountain pass into the Plain of Arafat. They spend the night at a place called Mina in prayer and meditation and in visiting with each other. On the second day they proceed to the Hill of Arafat where the *wukuf,* or Standing, takes place. Here they stay from noon until sunset in supplication and perhaps hear a commemoration of Muhammad's farewell sermon calling for peace and harmony among all believers. After sunset the pilgrims move to another site on the plain called Muzdalifa, where they gather pebbles to stone the devil the next day and where they also spend the night as before. On the third day they return to Mina, where they throw their pebbles at a pillar representing the devil.

On the fourth day the feast of the Sacrifice (*Id al-Adha*) begins, when each head of household is expected to sacrifice an animal in memory of Abraham's willingness to sacrifice his son Ismail at God's command. Throughout the world Muslims make a similar sacrifice on this day. The meat is cooked, part of it is eaten and the rest is given to the poor. At this point the pilgrim may discard the ihram for his ordinary clothing, clip his nails and shave (women cut off a symbolic lock). They are now free to return to Mecca, where they usually make another ritual circling of the Ka'ba.

Most pilgrims visit Medina on their way to or from Mecca, although this is not part of the pilgrimage. There they pay their respects at Muhammad's tomb and visit the tombs of other members of his family and of his companions.

Until a few years ago, most pilgrims traveled to Mecca by land, in huge caravans wending their way across the deserts surrounding the Holy City, or by ship crossing the Red Sea. These caravans assembled months ahead at such points as Damascus, Cairo and Baghdad and gathered together pilgrims from Turkey and eastern Europe, North Africa and Sudan, Iran, Samarkand and India. The caravans were like moving cities, the pilgrims traveling by horse, camel, litter or on foot, combining all levels of society and many nationalities and races. The rulers of Muslim countries organized the caravans, appointed leaders and troops for their protection, supplied money and foodstuffs and built roads and water cisterns along the way. The entire voyage might take six months or a year, and many pilgrims died of hardship or disease.

> And proclaim the Pilgrimage
> Among men; they will come
> To thee on foot and mounted
> On every kind of camel,
> Lean on account of journeys
> Through deep and distant
> Mountain highways.... (Sura XXII)

Today the great majority of pilgrims come by air to Jiddah and travel the short distance to Mecca by road. The Saudi Arabian government has created a huge infrastructure for the pilgrimage, including a giant airport, reception centers, local transport, accommodations, water and food supplies and health facilities. In the mid-19th century the number of pilgrims in one year was estimated to be about 50,000. Today the number is nearly two million and growing every year. The pilgrims come from every continent and nearly every country in the world, their travel facilitated by the recently recovered independence of many Muslim states, by greater wealth and by improved transport. The Hajj remains one of the most striking manifestations of religious faith and unity in the world today.

3
THE LAW

The most highly developed form of Islamic thought is the Law. Under Islam the Law is of divine origin, transmitted from God through Muhammad. It recognizes no difference between the religious and the secular and governs every aspect of the believer's life. Consequently, the most acute and creative minds in the Muslim world have been devoted to elaborating the basic Law, as expounded in the Quran and the Hadith, into a structure of intricate and harmonious design. The central role of the Holy Law of Islam is summed up in the Arabic name for it, *Shari'a,* "the path to the watering place."

The Islamic state was founded by God, and the caliph or head of state rules under God and is obliged to impose the Holy Law. The Shari'a, in theory, is infallible and immutable doctrine regulating the whole of the religious, political, social and private life of believers and to a certain extent of nonbelievers living under Muslim rule. Its provisions cover a wide ground, including criminal law, oaths, contracts, evidence, judicial procedure, marriage, the family, inheritance, slavery, education, personal hygiene, killing of animals, even manners and deportment.

The Four Sources of Law

According to Sunni Islam there are four sources of Shari'a. First and foremost comes the Quran, the word of God. Second comes the Hadith, or traditions of the Prophet. Where these two sources are silent, Shari'a is derived from two human sources. *Ijma',* or consensus, is sanctioned by a hadith of Muhammad's saying that his community would not agree to error. In practice ijma' is the consensus not of the entire community but of the *ulama,* those learned in religion and the Law. *Qiyas* (analogy), the deduction of legal prescriptions from the Quran and the Hadith by reasoning from parallel cases, covers situations not treated in the Quran or by the Prophet. It is the last resort based on the intellect of man, a weak instrument compared to the word of God and the example of the Prophet. Together, ijma' and qiyas cover situations untreated in the Quran and the traditions of the Prophet.

Schools of Law

Within Sunni Islam there are four schools of Law, differing from one another on minor points of interpretation and procedure. All Sunni Muslims adhere to one or another of these four schools, each of which recognizes the jurisdiction of the other. They are named for their founders or codifiers.

The earliest school, called the Maliki School, was founded in Medina by Malik ibn Anas (718-96). It placed emphasis on tradition and produced the first law manual, still in use as a text. Today Malikites are predominant in Upper Egypt, North Africa and West Africa.

Meanwhile, another school was developing in Iraq, led by one Abu Hanifah (699-767). Concentrating more on juridical opinion and less on tradition, the Hanafi school introduced legal reasoning based on analogy (qiyas). It is found today chiefly in Turkey, western Asia, India and Lower Egypt.

The third school, the Shafi'i, is named after Muhammad ibn Idris al-Shafi'i (768-820), the greatest of all Muslim jurists, who founded the classical science of Islamic law (*fiqh* or "understanding"). He is the author of the first scientific treatment of Islamic law, which is still a recognized textbook. [Fiqh regards theology as a branch of jurisprudence and is the science that regulates man's relations not only with himself and his fellow men but also with God; it thus provides regulations in religious as well as secular matters, determining what is legally permitted (*halal*) and what is legally prohibited (*haram*).] The Shafi'ites are represented in Syria, Lower Egypt, India and Indonesia.

The fourth orthodox school, the Hanbali, is the smallest and most conservative. It was founded by Ahmad ibn Hanbal (d. 855), who studied in Baghdad under al-Shafi'i. The Hanbalites reject ijma' and strictly follow the Quran and tradition. Adherents of this school today are the Wahhabis of Saudi Arabia.

Shi'a, the dissident branch of Islam, developed its own schools. Its followers reject ijma', adhere to the infallibility of their Imam and have their own laws, jurists and theologians.

Moral Basis

According to Islamic law, the acts of man fall into one of five moral categories. These are: (1) the obligatory, or actions which are rewarded if performed and punished if neglected; (2) the meritorious but not obligatory, or voluntary acts which are rewarded if performed but not punished if omitted; (3) indifferent, or actions which are morally neutral and attract neither reward nor punishment; (4) acts which are disapproved but not forbidden (divorce falls into this category according to some schools); and (5) the forbidden, or acts which are punishable by Allah and state. There are further divisions and intermediate grades between the five categories.

Legal Procedure

Cases which come before a Shari'a court are heard by a *qadi*, a religious judge appointed by the state. He hears the testimony of the plaintiff, the defendant and their witnesses. Normally none of these parties is placed under oath; only in cases of irreconcilable evidence are they asked by the qadi if they are willing "to take the oath," and they are at liberty to refuse. The testimony of a Muslim known to be exact in his religious duties outweighs that of one who is not, that of any Muslim outweighs that of a non-Muslim, and that of a man outweighs that of a woman.

Enforcement

The decisions of the qadi are enforced if necessary by the state. In criminal cases, the punishments in Western eyes are a curious mixture of the lenient and the severe. For homicide or wounding, for example, the punishment is not necessarily execution or imprisonment but the payment of *diya,* or blood money. This was an ancient custom of the Arabs, designed to reduce or eliminate the practice of blood feuds which caused further killings or woundings. The scale of payment is graded according to the status of the parties, the intention of the antagonist and the seriousness of the crime. Punishments which dismay Westerners, such as the stoning of an adultress or the chopping off of the hand of a thief, belong to an earlier era much harsher than today. They are rarely invoked in the present day and then only in a few very conservative countries, where motivation for a crime is also taken into account. An inveterate thief, for example, who steals solely for greed and personal gain may be punished severely; the first offender who steals to feed his hungry family may be punished lightly or not at all.

Practice

All of the foregoing describes the status and functioning of the Law in the ideal Islamic state. In practice, Muslim thinkers agree that this ideal state has hardly ever existed, perhaps only under the first four caliphs. From the time of the Umayyads the authorities found that they had to square Shari'a with the practical problems of governing areas with widely different conditions and traditions. This they did by creating a system of independent regulations called *qanun* and of separate courts to administer it. An attempt was made not to draw too sharp a line between Qanun and Shari'a but often the administrative law evaded or even set aside the provisions of Shari'a. In effect a system of secular law grew up alongside that of sacred law, and it gradually took over most of the latter's functions except in the fields of religion, the family and inheritance. During the 19th century, as part of its program of modernization, the Ottoman government openly introduced civil codes based on European models, first in the realm of commercial law and then in penal law. In modern times most Islamic states have followed suit. Even Saudi Arabia, which still adheres to the Shari'a, has supplemented it with regulations in the fields of public health, customs, commerce and labor.

4
MUHAMMAD AND ISLAM'S ORIGINS

Unlike most of the major religions of the world, Islam was born into the reasonably clear light of recent times. It originated in the seventh century A.D., and its prophet, Muhammad, was not only a conveyor of the word of God, but also a brilliant military and political leader whose actions and decisions changed the course of history. As with most charismatic persons, legends gathered around him, but the main facts of his life are well known.

Muhammad was born about 570 in the town of Mecca, in the territory known as the Hijaz on the west coast of Arabia. Mecca was a commercial center for the caravan trade, which transported goods from India and further east to the Mediterranean world. The Prophet of Islam was therefore raised in an urban community with links to the centers of contemporary civilization and not in the simple pastoral world of the desert Bedouin, as is sometimes thought. Mecca also had the distinction of being a religious center for centuries before the coming of Islam. It had long contained a shrine, called the Ka'ba, dedicated to several gods and goddesses under a chief deity called Allah. This shrine attracted many Arabs to an annual pilgrimage and fair, which brought rich profits into Mecca.

Though related to the Quraish, one of the ruling clans of the city, Muhammad's immediate family was poor and he was orphaned early in life. He was brought up at first by his grandfather and then by an uncle. As was common among city Arabs, the boy was sent to live for two years with a Bedouin family to benefit from the healthy outdoor life and to learn the frugal ways and self-reliance of the desert Arabs. While still young, Muhammad went to work for Khadija, a wealthy widow engaged in the caravan trade.

It is thought that he accompanied caravans along the roads of Arabia and perhaps into Syria, and that in the course of his travels he met people who greatly influenced his religious inclinations. In Bosra in southern Syria he is said to have met and listened to a Christian monk called Bahira, who saw in the boy signs of his coming prophet-hood.

In Yathrib (later to be called Medina), a caravan town 280 miles north of Mecca, he may have come into contact with Jews who dominated the commercial life there. He must have known Christians from Syria and Persia, who lived in some of the oasis towns and came to Mecca for the fair and pilgrimage. Several northern Arabian tribes had been converted to Christianity, and there was a school of native monotheists called Hanif, who were neither Jewish nor Christian but who rejected the polytheism prevalent in Arabia. Through such contacts Muhammad must have absorbed a great deal of Old and New Testament lore and become strongly impressed by the fact that both Jews and Christians possessed written scriptures.

At about the age of twenty-five, Muhammad married his employer Khadija, who was fifteen years older than he.

From all accounts they were a loving pair and, although polygamy was common in Arabia, he did not marry again in her lifetime. They produced several children; their sons died young but four daughters survived and married men who were Muhammad's future supporters. One daughter, Fatima, married a young kinsman named Ali, whose followers played an important role in the future of Islam.

The First Revelation

Muhammad was always a religious man, deeply concerned about social injustice and the corruption of the religious establishment of Mecca. Often he spent the night in meditation and prayer in the mountains nearby. On one such night in the year 610, when he was in his early forties, a holy spirit (traditionally identified with the Archangel Gabriel) appeared to him and ordered, "Proclaim!" Muhammad answered, "What shall I proclaim?" The spirit commanded:

> Proclaim! In the name
> Of thy Lord and Cherisher,
> Who created—
> Created man, out of
> A mere clot
> Of congealed blood:
> Proclaim! And thy Lord
> Is most Bountiful—
> He who taught
> The use of the Pen
> Taught man that
> Which he knew not (Sura XCVI)

At first he told only his wife of this event and of subsequent messages which the angel brought him. Khadija, believing in him implicitly, sustained him by her support and faith. Soon, however, the angel commanded him to proclaim publicly what had been revealed to him. Muhammad at first had no intention of creating a new religion. He wished only to call men to a belief in one God, Allah, to teach them to seek God's forgiveness for their sins, to help those in need and to lead better lives.

Muhammad clearly had the kind of personality that inspired affection and trust. Gibbon in *The Decline and Fall of the Roman Empire* described him thus: "According to the tradition of his companions, Muhammad was distinguished by the beauty of his person.... Before he spoke the orator engaged on his side the affections of a public and private audience. They applauded his commanding presence, his majestic aspect, his piercing eye, his gracious smile, his flowing beard, his countenance that painted every sensation of the soul, and his gestures that enforced each expression of the tongue.... His memory was capacious and retentive; his wit easy and social; his imagination sublime; his judgment clear, rapid, and decisive. He possessed the courage of both thought and action; and, although his designs might gradually expand with his success, the first idea which he entertained of his divine mission bears the stamp of an original and superior genius."

Early Converts

Muhammad's first converts were among the poor, the young and the enslaved. Among the earliest, besides his wife Khadija, were Abu Bakr, a friend and his future father-in-law, and Ali, a cousin and future son-in-law. Another was

Bilal, an Abyssinian slave, whom Muhammad made his first muezzin, or caller to prayer.

The Meccan establishment, however, learned of these activities and feared Muhammad's doctrine of strict monotheism as a threat to their control of the Ka'ba and the profits of the pilgrimage as then constituted. They also believed that some of his social prescriptions challenged the status quo and were liable to invade the economic and political domain, thus creating real problems for the ruling powers of Mecca.

To discredit him, the Meccans accused Muhammad of fraud and of taking his ideas from foreigners (Christians and Jews) and began to persecute his followers. Muhammad, protected by his connection with the powerful Quraish clan, was able to continue. But he sent about a hundred of his people across the Red Sea to safety in Abyssinia. There the tolerance and hospitality of the Christian inhabitants disposed early Islam toward affection and respect for Christianity.

Despite persecution, the number of Muslims increased. One of the most important converts was Omar ibn al-Khattab, a man of high standing in the community who later became the second of Muhammad's successors. These early Muslims came to be honored with the title *al-sahaba,* or Companions of the Prophet. In 619, however, Muhammad's uncle and protector died, as well as his helpmeet Khadija. Mourning his loss and seeking a more receptive community, Muhammad retired to the town of Taif. There his message again met with insult and mockery and he was stoned by a mob. In despair he returned to Mecca; but before entering the city he obtained the protection of another kinsman and married another widow, Sa'uda. He also became engaged to Aisha, a young daughter of Abu Bakr. Aisha, as Muhammad's favorite wife of his later years, was also to play a prominent part in the future of Islam as a source of traditions concerning the Prophet and also in the battle for succession after his death.

The Nocturnal Journey

During this difficult period Muhammad had an experience, which seemed to outsiders to have been a dream, but to himself and his followers was a reality. The event is described in the Quran thus:

> Glory to God
> Who did take His Servant
> For a Journey by Night
> From the Sacred Mosque
> To the Farthest Mosque
> Whose precincts we did
> Bless.... (Sura XVII)

This passage is believed by Muslims to refer to the Nocturnal Journey when, in the course of a single night, Muhammad was summoned by God to travel from Mecca to Jerusalem and thence into Heaven and back to Mecca. The journey was made on the back of a fabulous beast called Buraq. On reaching Jerusalem, Muhammad met and prayed with the prophets of the past, including Abraham, Moses and Jesus, at the place where the Dome of the Rock now stands. Accompanied by Gabriel, Muhammad then ascended a ladder of light through the seven stages of Heaven, where he met and conversed with angels and other heavenly beings. It is disputed among Muslims whether he actually stood before the throne of God, but he is thought to have received divine instructions concerning Islam. He then returned to Jerusalem and again mounting Buraq returned to Mecca before dawn. The Nocturnal Journey confirmed the prophethood of Muhammad and also established Jerusalem as one of the three holy cities of Islam.

The Hijra

A decisive change now occurred in Muhammad's fortunes. Some men from Yathrib who came on pilgrimage to Mecca were converted to Islam and returned home to convert others. For some time Yathrib had been torn apart by the violent rivalry of two powerful Arab tribes and their Jewish supporters. Muhammad, though still a prophet without honor in his own country, evidently so impressed his converts in Yathrib that they invited him to come and mediate between the warring factions. Seizing the opportunity, he sent two hundred of his followers ahead in small groups to avoid the suspicion of the Meccans. Then he and Abu Bakr slipped away. The Meccans sent out a search party, but the fugitives hid in a cave and eluded them.

In Yathrib the Prophet was given an enthusiastic welcome. The year of the flight was 622, known as Anno Hegira or A.H. from the Arabic word *hijra,* or "migration." Yathrib became known as the city of the Prophet, *Madinat al-Nabi,* or Medina for short.

The move to Medina was a fateful one in Muslim and world history. Almost at once Muhammad was transformed from the leader of a small and persecuted minority to the principal authority in an important Arabian town. As

Muhammad's influence spread, the religion and precepts of
✱ Islam as revealed to him became the basis for Medina's
governmental and social reformation. Soon after his arrival,
he drew up a charter binding all Muslims together in
fraternal loyalty. This was a revolutionary concept, as
hitherto the Arabs owed allegiance exclusively to their
family and their tribe. The revelations now received by
Muhammad in Medina began to contain detailed instructions on legal and social matters such as marriage, divorce,
dietary restrictions, taxes and the conduct of war. Under
the charter the Jews and Christians of Medina shared the
same privileges as "a community along with the Muslims"
and were allowed to keep their own religion, though
compelled to pay a special tax, approximately the Muslim's
zakah. Only pagans were beyond the pale and forced to
choose between Islam and the sword. This became the
pattern in all subsequent Muslim conquests and
settlements.

Conquest of Mecca

All the people of Medina, however, did not bow easily to
the new authority. The Jews rejected Muhammad's claim to
be a prophet in the line of the Old Testament and were
suspected of political treachery. The rivalry between the
Arab tribes of Medina smoldered, and new ones flared up
between his Meccan and Medinan followers. Muhammad
also had to contend with economic and social problems, as
the balance between nomadic and urban life was changing.
He needed great political skill and leadership to weld a
community of believers out of these discordant forces.

But it was still Muhammad's paramount desire to

convert the people of Mecca and to cleanse the Ka'ba of polytheism. Realizing that more than religious fervor and political skill were now needed, he pragmatically decided upon a course of action that would achieve both ends. To forestall attacks against his budding movement, he launched a series of preemptive raids on the rich caravans that flowed in and out of Mecca, thus striking a blow against both the political authority and economic power of Mecca.

In the first raid, made in 624 at a watering place called Badr, Muhammad himself led a force of 300 believers against a Quraish caravan defended by a thousand Meccans. The Muslims lost 14 men, the Meccans 70, in this first of the Muslim victories that changed the face of Arabia.

More attacks on Meccan caravans followed, and the issue was finally decided in a series of battles equally famous in Muslim history. In the Battle of Uhud the outnumbered Muslims were forced to retreat and Muhammad himself was slightly wounded. In the next battle a force of ten thousand Meccans, Jews and Bedouins marched on Medina. Muhammad ordered his men to dig deep trenches around the city, an innovative tactic in Arab warfare. Unwilling to risk casualties by negotiating the trench under fire, the Meccans futilely fired arrows at long range against the defenders. In this Battle of the Ditch only eight men were killed on both sides and the Meccans returned home in frustration.

Although this battle was not the last, the Quraish of Mecca signed a treaty with Muhammad which allowed the Muslims to attend the pilgrimage to the Ka'ba in exchange for a ten-year truce. Two years later, in 630, the Quraish broke the truce by attacking a tribe under Muhammad's protection. Muhammad then marched on Mecca at the head of 10,000 men, defeated the demoralized defenders with little loss of life and entered the city as a conqueror. Demanding the keys to the sanctuary, he ordered his men to destroy the images of the gods. He then entered to pray, thus assuring the Ka'ba as the central shrine of Islam.

Muhammad's Final Years

Muhammad returned to Medina in 630, where he remained until his death two years later. His powers showed no sign of weakening. He continued to receive revelations until almost his last day. From Medina he directed the campaigns of the Muslim armies which now ranged beyond the borders of Arabia into Byzantine territory. According to Muslim tradition the Prophet sent letters to the rulers of Byzantium, Persia and Abyssinia enjoining them to adopt Islam.

In the spring of 632, Muhammad made the pilgrimage to Mecca for the last time and his conduct on that occasion became the model for all future pilgrims. Returning to Medina, he planned an expedition against the Byzantines in Syria. But he fell ill of a fever and lay sick for three days, getting up only to attend prayers in the mosque. On the 8th of June 632, he died in Aisha's arms and was buried under the floor of her house.

Muhammad had succeeded in founding a religion, a state and an army as well as laying the groundwork of an empire; but he died leaving no heir or an appointed successor. The ensuing struggle for leadership played a large and fateful role in the future history of Islam.

5

SECTS: VARIATION IN BELIEF

As with Christianity and other major religions, the original unity of Islam was soon broken. The big split, which lasts to this day, occurred during the generation following the death of Muhammad. It left the Muslim world divided into two major groups, the Sunna and the Shi'a.

The Sunna

Sunnis comprise 85-90 percent of the body of Muslims and adhere to the basic beliefs and practices of Islam as outlined in the preceding chapters.

The Shi'a

Shi'ites comprise 10-15 percent of the Muslim faith. They are divided into many different sects all more or less at variance with one another as well as with the Sunnis. Shi'ites form a majority in Iran and Yemen and have important minorities in Iraq, Syria, Lebanon, Eastern Arabia and parts of India.

The origin of the split was political rather than religious. When Muhammad died without an heir the Muslims

gathered to elect a caliph ("successor") to replace him. All
the candidates were related to Muhammad by marriage
and one, his cousin Ali ibn Abu Talib, by blood as well.
Many supporters considered Ali's claim to be the strongest,
since he was married to Muhammad's favorite daughter,
Fatima. In rivalry, however, was Aisha, the Prophet's young
and childless widow, who succeeded in assuring the
election of her father Abu Bakr as the first caliph. Abu Bakr,
who had been Muhammad's close friend, held the Muslim
community together and presided over the expansion of
Islam throughout Arabia. When he died two years later,
Omar ibn al-Khattab, another of Muhammad's fathers-in-
law, was elected second caliph, again with the support of
Aisha and against the opposition of Ali. Omar was a strong
leader, who directed the Muslim invasion of Syria and
Egypt, established the judiciary system and changed the
simple patriarchalism of Islam into something resembling
an imperial government. Ten years later he was killed by a
slave over a tax dispute, although his supporters suspected
a conspiracy among his rivals.

The third caliph, Uthman ibn Affan, was chosen as a
compromise candidate in 645 over the opposition of both
Ali and Aisha. Muhammad's father-in-law twice over,
Uthman had been a late convert to Islam and played only a
minor role in its early history, although he was a member
of the rich and powerful Umayyad branch of the Quraish
clan of Mecca. In the eleventh year of his reign rebellion
broke out in Iraq and Egypt; and when the Egyptians
marched on his capital at Medina, Uthman was killed.

Ali was finally elected caliph in 656. But Aisha did not
accept his election and joined a party of dissident Meccans

to oppose him. They attacked Ali at the Battle of the Camel, so-called because Aisha encouraged her allies from the back of a camel on the sidelines. Despite her efforts, Ali won the battle and sent Aisha back to Medina under escort.

Meanwhile, Mu'awiya ibn Abu Sufyan, governor of Syria, led a force against Ali to avenge the death of his uncle Uthman. Ali appeared to be winning the Battle of Siffin in Iraq, when Mu'awiya ordered his men to tie copies of the Quran to the points of their lances and to cry, "Let Allah decide." Ali agreed to submit to arbitration, but when the mediators voted against him he refused to accept their decision. By submitting to arbitration in the first place, however, Ali offended a fanatical band of his followers, who withdrew into northern Iraq. Known as the Kharijites, or "Seceders," they rose in rebellion against Ali. In 661, when Ali was assassinated by a Kharijite, Mu'awiya was proclaimed caliph in Jerusalem and founded the Umayyad dynasty. Damascus became the new capital of Islam, thus removing the caliphate from Arabia forever. Regarded as one of the political geniuses of Islam, Mu'awiya modernized the state and made it into an empire.

> "I apply not my lash where my tongue suffices, nor my sword where the whip is enough. And if there is one hair binding me to my fellow men, I let it not break. If they pull I loosen, and if they loosen I pull."
>
> —Caliph Mu'awiya

Shi'at 'Ali, "the party of Ali," however, did not die with its leader. On the contrary it grew larger with the adherence of all those at odds with the Umayyads. Hasan, the older son of Ali and Fatima, died a few years after the death of his father, poisoned according to Shi'ite belief by his enemies. His brother Husain, on the death of Mu'awiya in 680, came under a truce to discuss peace, and was attacked and slain by the Umayyads at Karbala in Iraq. His tomb there has become a great Shi'ite shrine and center of pilgrimage.

The question of the succession to the caliphate conceals a deep philosophical difference within Islam. The Sunnis believe in ijma', the consensus of the Islamic community through which God reveals His will. The community is therefore empowered to elect the caliph, who could be any devout believer with the proper qualifications to rule. The Shi'ites on the other hand restrict eligibility for the caliphate to the descendants of the Prophet through Ali and Fatima. They are royalists, believing in the divine right of the Alids to be caliphs—or Imams as they call them—of Islam.

In the more extreme Shi'ite sects, this stance became elaborated into a theory that the Imam inherits a divine light by virtue of his descent, not only from Muhammad and Ali, but from all the prophets beginning with Adam.

Because of its opposition to the established authorities, Shi'a attracted all sorts of religious non-conformists. Many of the new converts to Islam brought with them ideas and practices from the older religions of the Middle East. They reconciled these with the Quran by giving to the suras an esoteric interpretation to be understood only by the initiated.

For example, the idea of the Holy Family is very ancient in the religions of the Middle East. In Shi'ite Islam, the Holy Family is incarnated in Muhammad, Ali, Fatima and their sons Hasan and Husain. The "martyrdom" of Ali and his sons fed this image. Fatima became the ideal woman and quasi-divine. Intercession between men and God, an idea condemned in Sunni Islam, is one of the functions of the Holy Family.

Another doctrine prevalent in the Middle East is that of metempsychosis, the transmigration of souls. Extreme Shi'ites believe in this, both in the sense of migration of the soul from one body to another and in the sense of incarnation of the divine in all or certain men. Numerology also plays a role in Shi'ite Islam, with the number seven being particularly sacred.

A concept common to most branches of the Shi'a is that of the Hidden Imam. They believe that one of the historical Imams did not die but disappeared and remains in hiding. The sects disagree as to which of the historical Imams this was, but the idea remains the same. Meanwhile his authority is maintained on earth by his representatives, who have constant contact with him and receive his instructions. At the end of time, the Hidden Imam will reappear as the *mahdi* ("The Guided One"), who will establish peace and justice on earth. Throughout history various political leaders preaching nationalism and Islamic reform have claimed to be the Mahdi.

The belief in the Hidden Imam and the Mahdi probably stems from the feeling among the Shi'ites that they have been denied their rights in this world. The descendants of Ali have not come into their own as rulers of the entire Islamic world and many of them have died what their supporters hold to be martyrs' deaths. In particular the Shi'ites commemorate the martyrdom of Husain with passion plays and self-laceration by the faithful. There is thus an element of tragedy in Shi'ite Islam which is not found in Sunni Islam. For the followers of Ali the world has been a place of violence, martyrdom and tragedy.

Variations in Sunni Islam

Before discussing the major Shi'ite sects, it is appropriate to consider the earliest of all Islamic sects, the **Kharijites,** who split from Ali and later killed him. They held that the only test for a true Muslim is purity of conduct and belief and that those who did not pass the test were infidels. Although they lost power as a sect in the 8th century, Kharijites exist today in isolated groups in North Africa, southern Arabia and on the east coast of Africa. They played an important part in the development of Muslim theology and had a strong influence on the Wahhabi movement, one of the most recent off-shoots of Sunni Islam.

The **Wahhabis** adhere more strictly to the fundamental beliefs and practices of Islam than other Muslims. The movement was founded in the mid-18th century in the heart of Arabia by Muhammad ibn Abd al-Wahhab, a teacher who had traveled and studied widely in Iraq and Iran, as well as in Arabia. He condemned much of what he saw in contemporary Islam as "polytheism" (especially the worship of local saints) and called on his followers to return to the traditions of early Islam. The Wahhabis call themselves *muwahhidun* ("Unitarian") and belong to the conservative Hanbali School of Law. Allied with the House of Sa'ud, they gained control of most of Arabia in the early 19th century. After a period of temporary decline under the Ottomans, the Wahhabis re-emerged in the 20th century under Ibn Sa'ud, the founder of Saudi Arabia. Their conservative interpretation of Islamic doctrine governs that state today.

Major Shi'ite Sects

Of the major Shi'ite sects which have emerged over the centuries, many have disappeared; others have subdivided many times. We will discuss here only a few of the major sects still in existence.

The largest Shi'ite sect is the **Ithna Ashariya,** or "Twelvers," so called because they recognize Twelve Imams, all descendants of Ali. The last Imam was Muham-mad al-Mahdi who, his followers believe, disappeared into hiding in 878 to return to rule again one day. The Twelvers are the dominant branch of Islam in present-day Iran, where the sect became the state religion in the 15th century. Twelvers are also found in Iraq, Syria, Lebanon, Morocco and India. They add the name of Ali to the Shahada, or profession of faith, and beseech the Holy Family for their intercession with Allah. The Twelve Imams guard and direct the destiny of the world, and pilgrimages are made to their tombs.

The **Sab'iya,** or "Seveners," restrict the number of Imams to seven, but the different sub-groups in the sect disagree as to which caliphs are included among them.

Among the branches of this sect are the **Ismailis,** who take their name from the man they consider to be the seventh Imam. In the 11th century, Ismaili followers spread their faith from the Atlantic to India and threatened the hegemony of Sunni Islam. Ismailis came to power in Egypt under the Fatimids (969 to 1171) and in Arabia under the

Qarmatians, who swept across the peninsula in the 10th century, sacking Mecca and Medina and taking the Black Stone from the Ka'ba back to their home on the Arabian Gulf. Other descendants of the Ismailis still live quietly in the mountains of Syria under the name **Nusairi** which includes the **Alawites,** the present ruling party of Syria. Today, the Ismailis of Persia and India are the prosperous and energetic followers of the Agha Khan.

The **Zaidis** of Yemen are the Shi'ite sect closest to Sunni Islam. Although they believe that the Imam must be a descendant of Ali, they do not believe in a Hidden Imam, since the leader of the faithful must be able to defend the faith here in this world.

Other Variations in Islam

Several other tendencies in Islam add to the variety of the Muslim world.

The **Sufis** are the mystics of Islam and are divided into many sects and schools. The name "sufi" comes from the Arabic name for wool, possibly related to the woolen robes worn by Christian monks. All Sufis share a belief that mystical union with God and perfect understanding can be reached by the practice of certain disciplines. The basis of Sufism is a communal life organized under a charismatic leader. These fraternities teach a *tariqa*, or way, which leads through several stages to detachment from material things and to the ultimate truth. The principal ritual of the Sufis is *dhikr*, "remembering" God, through endless repetition of religious phrases leading to selfhypnosis. Fasting, dancing, the use of drums and stimulants also help to produce a trance-like state. The philosophical basis of Sufism is a kind of pantheism, the belief that God is immanent in creation rather than transcendent to it. The individual is part of God and the truth consists in realizing this. Sufism was always strongest among non-Arabs and has recently attracted many people in the West.

The **Marabouts** of North Africa represent a cult of local saints which has survived alongside Islam despite the Quranic ban on saints. Many Marabouts were historical men and women noted for their piety, learning, or power of healing or performing miracles; others seem to be the remnants of local nature cults. Saints and their sanctuaries are venerated in other parts of the Muslim world, especially among the Shi'ites.

The **Black Muslim** movement, founded by Afro-Americans in the United States as a protest against racism, stresses the Islamic principles of universal brotherhood and social justice. They are a minority, however, among American Muslims, which today number four million.

The **Druze** were originally an offshoot of Ismaili Islam, but today neither Muslims nor the Druze themselves consider this group to be part of the Islamic faith. Since they no longer accept converts and keep their doctrine secret, any description of their religious beliefs and prac- tices must be speculative. It is known that the Druze believe in one God who has reappeared in as many as seventy incarnations. Al-Hakim, sixth Fatimid caliph in Cairo (966–1020), was the final incarnation and supreme deity, and he will reappear to conquer the world. The Gospel and the Quran are accepted as inspired books, but only special Druze scriptures are regarded as supreme religious guides.

The Druze are concentrated in the mountains of Lebanon and Syria, with a scattering among the Kurds and Turks.

The **Bahai** and the **Ahmadi** are considered heretical sects, who broke away from Islam. The Bahai were founded in Iran in the mid-19th century on a platform of humanitarianism, pacifism and universalism; they have recently come into conflict with the revivalism of the Iranian revolution. In India at the turn of the century Ahmad al-Qadiani founded the Ahmadi sect, claiming that he was the manifestation of Muhammad, Jesus, and the Hindu god Krishna. The sect claims to have over a million members in southeast Asia and Africa.

6

THE SPREAD OF ISLAM

Islam spread with astonishing rapidity out of Arabia and into a large part of the known world. Within ten years of Muhammad's death, the forces of Islam had conquered all of Greater Syria, Iraq and Egypt. Eighty years later, Islam had become dominant over a broad band of territory embracing millions of people from the Atlantic and the Pyrenees in the west to the borders of India in the east. Subsequent waves of expansion were to carry Islam northward into Anatolia and the steppes of central Asia, southward into equatorial Africa, eastward across India and Indonesia into China and to the fringes of the Pacific, and northwest into the Balkans. In later years, Islam retreated from the Iberian peninsula and most of the Balkans, and for several centuries it was in political eclipse everywhere; but on the whole the great mass of people in the areas of its ascendancy has remained faithful to the Islamic faith.

It is a mistake to think that the success of Islam was due solely to armed conquest. The Arabs, who carried the first wave of expansion, did not compel the peoples they conquered to become Muslims. On the contrary, they considered themselves a ruling elite and discouraged conversions that would reduce revenues from taxes and tribute imposed on their non-Muslim subjects. Nevertheless, many thousands of Christians, Zoroastrians and Jews embraced Islam, partly no doubt through sincere belief, but also because of the access to wealth and power open only to Muslims. The later waves of Islamic expansion were due not so much to the conquest by Muslims of other peoples but to the conquest by other peoples of the Muslims. The Turks and Mongols, who entered the Middle East as conquerors, subsequently adopted the religion of their subjects and in turn spread it among their kinsmen in central Asia. In India the Mughals were already Muslims when they conquered the northern areas and they remained a minority ruling class. Also, many Hindus embraced Islam to escape the caste system. The gradual Islamization of Africa, Malaysia and Indonesia was the work of peaceful missionaries and traders.

To return to the Arabs, their rapid conquest of the Persian and Byzantine empires was the result of military skill inspired by religious zeal. Muhammad had divided the world into two realms, *dar al-Islam,* the abode of Islam, and *dar al-harb,* the abode of war, and had preached the doctrine of *jihad,* or holy struggle. Under the banner of Islam and with superb generalship, the Arab campaigns turned from border raids into the permanent occupation of the more fertile lands to the north. But the ease of the Arab conquest was also due to the nature of the enemy. The Persian and Byzantine empires had worn each other out in a long series of wars and had alienated their subjects by harsh government, heavy taxation and the persecution of local religious sects. The Arab conquests were facilitated by the cooperation of a sympathetic populace.

Early Conquests (632-655)

Under the first caliphs the Muslims conquered the whole of the Arabian Peninsula, Iraq, Persia, Syria and Lower Egypt. The victors established garrison towns on the edges of the desert and governed their new territories as a small military elite. They recognized and protected the Jews and Christians and allowed them in general to retain their property and to administer their own affairs. Certain lands were appropriated to the new state but private property was respected. These policies, established in all lands conquered by the Arabs, were welcomed by the subject people as a milder form of government than that of their former rulers.

The first four caliphs—Abu Bakr, Omar, Uthman and Ali—were elected to the position and are known as the *Khalifa al-Rashidoun* (The Wise Caliphs). Beginning with the Umayyads, succession to the Caliphate became a matter of inheritance within the family.

The Umayyads (661-750)

The Umayyad caliphs, the first of the Arab dynasties, continued the expansion of Islam from their capital in Damascus. The Arab armies were welcomed by the Berbers of North Africa, who were weary of the alternative tyrannies of Byzantines and Vandals, and in Spain, which was chafing under the harsh rule of the Visigoths. The Umayyads also pushed Islam eastward into Afghanistan

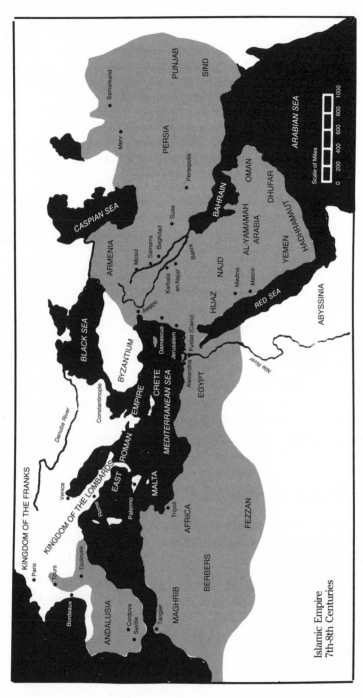

The tremendous extent of the Islamic empire of more than 1,000 years ago (above) bears a remarkable resemblance to the present areas of Islamic predominance (below), stretching from the Atlantic Ocean to the southwest Pacific.

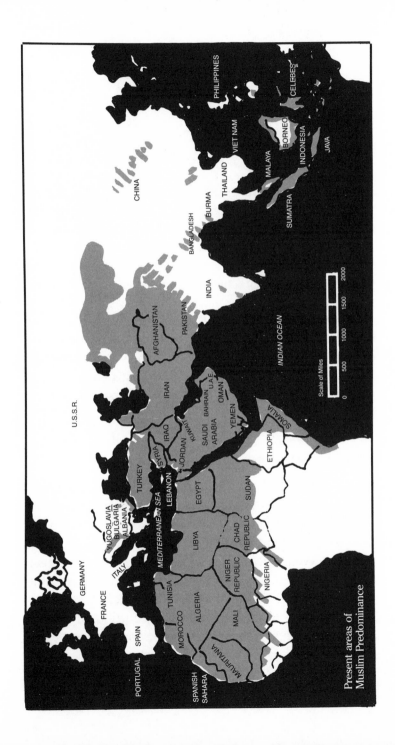

Present areas of
Muslim Predominance

and up to the banks of the Indus. Under them the Arab empire reached its greatest extent.

The Abbasids (762-1258)

But the Umayyads were under constant pressure, first from the partisans of Ali, murdered in 661 over a power struggle for the caliphate, and second from the *mawali,* non-Arab, mostly Persian, converts to Islam, who demanded the same status and privileges as the Arabs. Both groups supported the Abbasids, descendants of Muhammad's uncle Abbas, who overthrew the Umayyads in 750 and assumed leadership of the Islamic empire. The Abbasids established their capital at Baghdad, facing eastward toward Persia, and were exposed to increasing Persian influence. Although they reigned in Baghdad until 1258, the Abbasids soon came to rule in name only, as political power passed to various Persian warlords.

Rival Caliphates

In fact, the Arab Islamic empire was breaking up everywhere. In Egypt, an Iraqi general seized political power, but continued to recognize the Abbasids as caliphs. So did the Arab and Berber amirates that arose in North Africa and later carried Islam into Sicily and other Mediterranean islands. In Spain, an Umayyad prince, escaping from the general slaughter of his family after their defeat, set up an independent amirate. The Shi'ites contributed to the dissolution of the Arab empire by declaring their independence in northern Iraq, Yemen and central Arabia.

But the main challenge to Muslim unity arose in Tunis, where a man claiming descent from Ali and Fatima (the Prophet's daughter), appeared in 909 and declared himself caliph. Known as the Fatimids, this dynasty conquered Egypt in 969 and founded the city of Cairo. For two centuries they controlled Egypt, most of North Africa, Syria and Palestine, and the west coast of Arabia including the two holy cities of Mecca and Medina. Their assumption of the caliphate prompted the Umayyad amir of Cordova to declare himself caliph, and for a time there were three rival caliphs—Abbasid, Fatimid and Umayyad.

Despite these vicissitudes at the top, Islam continued to consolidate its hold over the people. Christianity disappeared entirely from two large areas, North Africa and the Arabian Peninsula, while in other places it dwindled, along with Judaism and Zoroastrianism, to a mere remnant of its former size. The history of this mass conversion is not clear, though it does not appear to have been the result of persecution or force. In Spain the Mozarabs—Arabized Christians and Jews—remained a distinct portion of the population and contributed greatly to Islamic culture. The gradual reconquest of Spain by Christian forces, however, began as early as the 9th century, culminating in the expulsion of all Muslims and Jews from the peninsula at the end of the 15th century.

The Seljuk Turks

Now a new ethnic element entered the Islamic heartland, one that was to carry Islam further into new areas east and west. During the 10th and 11th centuries, certain Turkish tribes migrated from their home in central Asia into the areas around the Caspian and the Black Seas. They were excellent soldiers and many of them entered the armies of local Muslim rulers as military slaves. One such Turkish tribe, the Seljuks, founded an independent sultanate which, while recognizing the religious authority of the Abbasid caliphs, claimed political and military control over the whole of Sunni Islam. They, and other Turkish converts, carried Islam to their brethren in central Asia and northern India, as well as into the western half of Asia Minor, where they expelled the Byzantines. On the eve of the Crusades in 1090, the Seljuk Turks ruled over Persia, Syria, Iraq, the West Coast of Arabia, the Punjab and Kashmir.

The Crusades

The Crusades were only a temporary setback in the history of Islam. Led by land-hungry Normans from France and financed by the merchant states of Italy, they were as much an economic venture as a religious campaign. In Muslim eyes, they were chiefly significant as the first armed incursion of Europe into Islamic lands and for having provoked animosity between Muslims and local Christians. In a contemporaneous development, the Normans permanently detached Sicily from the Muslim world and created a curious hybrid kingdom with both Christian and Muslim characteristics. In the Middle East, after about a century of Norman rule, a great Muslim general, Salah ad-Din al-Ayyubi (known as Saladin), drove the Crusaders out of the Holy Land and established his own dynasty in Cairo.

The Mongols

In the 13th century another pagan people from the heart of Asia burst upon the Islamic world. The Mongols, led by Genghis Khan's grandson Hulagu, shattered the Persians, sacked Baghdad, and put the Abbasid caliph to death. They destroyed the precious irrigation systems built by the Muslims and transported whole sections of the population to their eastern domains. The whole of southwest Asia was incorporated into their empire, ruled first from Mongolia and then from Peking. Later, certain Mongol tribes embraced Islam and founded two Muslim states—the Khanate of the Golden Horde and the Chaghatay Khanate—in central Asia, the remnants of which form part of the Soviet Union today.

The Mamluks

Meanwhile their cousins, the Turks, consolidated their hold over the former Arab and Byzantine lands. Baybars, a Turkish general of slave origin, ousted the Mongols from Syria and established a strange new dynasty, the Mamluks of Egypt. They had been the personal bodyguards of the Ayyubids, the dynasty founded by Saladin, boys bought or captured in the region around the Black Sea and trained as soldiers and administrators. After they seized power, they continued to maintain their numbers by importing young slaves from the Caucasus and Circassia, as well as from Turkish tribes. They brought the Abbasid caliph to Egypt and installed him as a powerless court official in Cairo. For over two centuries (1291-1517) the Mamluks ruled over

Egypt, Syria and western Arabia and created a brilliant Arab-Turkish civilization.

Ottoman Empire (1453-1921)

In the early 15th century, another Turkish group, the Ottomans or followers of Osman, advanced into Byzantine territory encircling Constantinople from their base at Ankara. At the request of the Byzantine emperor himself, they crossed into Europe to repress a revolt in the Balkans and then refused to leave. Bayazid, the Ottoman sultan, laid siege to Constantinople but was attacked and defeated in 1402 by another Mongol chief from the East, Tamurlane. The Ottomans soon recovered their fortunes, however, and in 1453 Mehmed II, known as the Conqueror, captured Constantinople and ended the thousand-year rule of Byzantium, thus fulfilling a prediction by the Prophet. On the death of the last Abbasid caliph, the Ottoman sultan assumed the title himself. Step by step the Ottomans created a powerful and the most longlived of Islamic empires. It lasted until 1921, including at its height Anatolia, Syria, Palestine, Egypt, Libya, Tunisia, Algeria, the Hijaz, Yemen, the Crimea, Greece, Cyprus, Crete, Bulgaria, Rumania, Yugoslavia, and parts of Hungary.

Persia

Through constant struggle, Persia was able to resist the embrace of the Ottomans. A Shi'ite dynasty, the Safavids, came to power in the mid-15th century and made Shi'ite Islam the official religion of Persia, which it remains today. Later the country was occupied by Afghans, until the emergence of the Qajars, who ruled from 1779 to 1923, when they were overthrown by the grandfather of the last shah, deposed in 1979. Persia was renamed Iran in 1935.

India

Although the Arabs invaded India as early as 711, the first Muslim dynasty to rule there for long (998-1030) was the Ghaznavid, founded by a Turkish slave. The Mongols under Tamurlane invaded India in 1398, leaving the Muslim area broken up into separate states. A century later Babur, who claimed descent on his father's side from Tamurlane and on his mother's from Genghis Khan, invaded Delhi and Rajputana and founded the first Mughal dynasty. His descendants extended and consolidated Muslim rule, although only ten percent of the population professed Islam. During the 18th century the Mughals gradually lost parts of their domain to the French and the English and to native rulers backed by the two European rivals. The Mughal state was finally dismantled by the British after the Indian Mutiny of 1857-58.

Decline and Resurgence

The age of European imperialism gradually extinguished Muslim political power throughout the world. The Ottomans were driven out of the Balkans; Russia pushed back the Mongols and annexed their territory; the British and the French carved up India; while the Dutch in Indonesia, the French in North Africa, and the British in Egypt, the Arabian Gulf and Iran either replaced the native rulers or imposed varying degrees of control over them. After World

War I, the Ottoman empire was dismembered, the caliphate abolished, and the former Arab provinces brought under European tutelage. The situation was reversed, however, in the aftermath of World War II, when almost all Muslim states regained their independence, with the exception of Palestine and the Central Asian possessions of Russia.

During all these political upheavals, the great mass of Muslims did not abandon their religion. In fact, Islam became a rallying point of nationalist resistance to the colonial powers and it continued, even under foreign domination, to expand by peaceful means. During the 18th and 19th centuries, traveling Muslims carried the Quran into southeast Asia and deep into the continent of Africa. Islam, it seems, retains its appeal for a wide range of peoples of greatly differing races and cultures. Today Islam is the fastest growing religion in the world.

7

ISLAM AND JUDAISM

Islam is intimately connected with Judaism through the One God. Historically, the Arabs and Hebrews originated in roughly the same area, somewhere in the Arabian Peninsula. Their languages are closely related, both stemming from the same Semitic source. And both claim descent from a common ancestor, the Prophet Abraham—the Hebrews through his son Isaac, the Arabs through his son Ismail. If religious concepts are at least partly molded by common experience, it is not surprising that Judaism and Islam should bear such a close resemblance.

The Quran and the Torah

Although Muhammad believed that the Quran was revealed to him as the full and final word of God, he also believed that parts of the Old Testament (called the Torah) and the New were divinely inspired, and he directed his listeners to the two earlier scriptures for instruction concerning Islam. For this reason he called both Jews and Christians *ahl al-kitab* or "People of the Book" and offered them his protection and the freedom to worship as they pleased. So close was this relationship that, according to the Quran, both the Old and New Testaments foretold the coming of Muhammad as a prophet.

The Torah and the Quran share such basic theological concepts as monotheism, the omnipotence of God, the primacy of revelation and the coming Day of Judgment. In an early chapter of the Quran, Jews are referred to as "the children of Israil, whom Allah rescued from Pharaoh and whom He chose in His knowledge." In later suras, however, the Quran accuses them of having broken their bond with Allah, of disagreeing among themselves and of distorting and falsifying the Torah, causing God to withdraw His protection from them.

Most strikingly, the Torah and the Quran share a great number of characters and incidents. The Quran, however, calls many of the Biblical characters—Adam, Noah, Lot, for example—prophets, which they are not in the Torah. In the Quran's creation story, Adam is formed from dried clay and softened by the rain; his wife Eve (Hawa) is made from his rib while he is sleeping. Allah orders the angels to bow down to Adam and all obey except Iblis, who, in revenge for his banishment from heaven, tempts Hawa to eat the fruit of the tree of knowledge. According to tradition, she in turn tempts Adam, first with wine and then with fruit; thus wine is the root of all evil. After expulsion from the garden, they become separated, Adam going to Ceylon where after 200 years of repentance he is rescued by the angel Gabriel and taken to Mecca. There he is reunited with Hawa and is taught the rites of the pilgrimage. The Quran also tells the story of Kabil (Cain) and Habil (Abel) and of a third son, Shith (Seth), who collected the revelations of Allah for Adam.

In the Quran Ibrahim (Abraham) was the first Muslim and was called "the Friend of God." The offer to sacrifice Ismail (Ishmael) and the quarrel between him and his brother Ishak (Isaac) and their mothers is related. Muslims believe that Ibrahim offered to sacrifice Ismail, not Ishak. Ibrahim takes Ismail and Hagar, his wife, to Arabia, where they dig new foundations for the Ka'ba. When Ibrahim leaves them, Ismail and Hagar wander in the desert until the angel Jibril (Gabriel) reveals to them the underground spring of Zamzam, which still flows beside the Ka'ba. The traditional sites of the tombs of Ismail and Hagar lie in the courtyard surrounding the Ka'ba.

Other Biblical characters who appear in the Quran are Jacob (Yaqub), Joseph (Yusuf), Moses (Musa), Solomon (Sulaiman), the Queen of Sheba (Belqis), David (Dawud), Goliath (Jalut), Saul (Talut), Job (Ayyub), Jonah (Yunus), and Joshua (Yasha). Their stories are basically the same as those in the Old Testament, though differing in detail.

This feeling of kinship with the Jews led Muhammad to expect them to accept him as a prophet and to support his mission. In the charter he drew up in Medina, he included the Jews as "a community among the Muslims." Some Jews of Medina, however, refused to recognize him as a prophet and mocked him for what they considered to be a garbled version of their scripture. The revelations he received in Medina began to show increasing hostility to Jews who did not follow the Torah and worship of one God.

During the battles between the Muslims of Medina and the Quraish of Mecca, the Medinan Jews were suspected of treachery by Muhammad, and in consequence he expelled two Jewish tribes from the city. In the subsequent battles for control of Mecca, Jewish opposition to Muhammad continued, provoking more severe punishment. After Islam reigned over the Hijaz, the Jews were allowed to remain in possession of their lands, provided they paid half their produce to the Muslims.

Muhammad's treatment of the Jews of Medina was normal by the standards of his day and hardly harsh when viewed against such events as the massacre of the Canaanites by the Hebrews and that of the Muslims and Jews of Jerusalem by the Crusaders. It was a question of disloyalty, not of race or religion, and is therefore not inconsistent with Islamic respect for "People of the Book."

Covenant of Jerusalem

The so-called Covenant of Omar with the people of Jerusalem, after the Muslim conquest of that city in 637, codified Muslim relations with the Jewish and Christian inhabitants. Those who submitted to the Muslims became *dhimma,* people of the covenant. This provided them with the unconditional protection of the Muslim authorities, permitted all Jews and Christians freedom of worship, control of their own property, management of their own communal affairs, and the right to repair and rebuild their places of worship. In return the dhimmas had to pay poll and land taxes. Pogroms against the Jews were almost unheard of in Islam, with the notorious exception of that conducted in Cairo in the 13th century by the mad Caliph al-Hakim, who went on to persecute the Muslims as well. Both Jews and Christians were well integrated into Muslim society, and many of them rose to high positions in government and intellectual circles and made valuable contributions to Islamic civilization.

Importance of Jerusalem

Today, the quarrel between Israel and the Muslim states is largely political, but it has a religious side as well. This centers around the Muslim claim to the city of Jerusalem, which enshrines one of the three holy sites of Islam.

Muhammad first made Jerusalem the *qibla,* or direction of prayer, for the Muslims. A later revelation changed this to the Ka'ba at Mecca, but Jerusalem remained important. Since the seventh century and Muhammad's Nocturnal Journey, the Holy City has been revered by all Muslims. These claims are reinforced by the Muslim belief in Abraham, other Old Testament prophets and Jesus, and hence the places associated with them are a part of Islam.

Muslim history glorified Jerusalem. When the Caliph Omar captured the city, he refused to pray at the Church of the Holy Sepulchre, as that would sanction its being turned into a mosque. Instead he asked to be shown to a site on Mount Moriah and was led to a huge bare rock covered with rubble and refuse. He ordered the place to be cleared and prayed there. In the years that followed, *al-Sakhra,* or Holy Rock, became of increasing importance in Islam. The Caliph Abd al-Malik erected in 691 a magnificent oratory over the Rock, known as *Qubbat al-Sakhra,* the Dome of the Rock. Here, in the enclosure, known to all Muslims as *al-Haram al-Sharif* or the Noble Sanctuary, he also built a mosque and named it *Masjid al-Aqsa,* the Farthest Mosque, after the Quranic verses of Muhammad's Nocturnal Journey. The Mosque, at various times through the ages, was destroyed by earthquake and fire and its structure is now almost entirely modern. But the Dome of the Rock, the golden-domed octagonal oratory built in the seventh century, is still much the same in its architectural splendor. It too suffered severe damage but was restored and embellished by subsequent Muslim rulers, most recently by King Hussein of Jordan in the 1960s.

Al-Sakhra

To Muslims, al-Sakhra means many things: it came originally from Paradise and angels visited it 2,000 years before the creation of Adam; it is closer to heaven than any other spot on earth and is guarded by angels; all sweet waters of the earth have their source under it; Noah's ark rested on the Rock after the flood had subsided, and here the angel Israfil will blow the last trumpet on the Day of Judgment. It is the spot from which Muhammad ascended into Heaven, and various mementoes of his presence—a handprint, a footprint, the spot from which he ascended—are pointed out to the faithful. Understandably, such associations make al-Sakhra, al-Haram al-Sharif and the whole of the Old City of Jerusalem of immutable holiness to Islam.

8
ISLAM AND CHRISTIANITY

The relation of Islam to Christianity resembles that of Christianity to Judaism. All three belong to the same family of monotheistic faiths, with each of the later creeds emerging from its predecessor. Neither Jesus nor Muhammad intended to create a new religion, but each thought of himself as developing and completing the old. Present-day Muslims are aware of the ties between their faith and Christianity and are surprised by a lack of information among modern Christians on this score.

Before the birth of Muhammad, the Christian gospels and Christian missionaries of different sects had penetrated the Arabian Peninsula. A Christian kingdom supported by the Ethiopians was set up in Yemen in 525, a generation before the birth of Muhammad. According to legend, the young Muhammad himself, when riding with the caravans from Mecca, met and talked with Christians in Arabia and southern Syria.

In the Quran

Jesus is named as one of the prophets in the Quran, but his character and achievements are of a different order from those of the other prophets. He was born of a virgin by the direct creative act of Allah. He could perform miracles—raising the dead, healing the sick, breathing life into clay birds—a gift denied even to Muhammad. In addition, Allah revealed to Jesus a sacred book called *Injil* (Evangel). Although Jesus had no earthly father, he was not the son of God and had no claim to divinity. "O People of the Book," one Quranic sura warns,

> Commit no excesses
> In your religion: nor say
> Of God aught but the truth.
> Christ Jesus the son of Mary
> Was no more than
> An apostle of God
> And his Word
> Which He bestowed on Mary,
> And a Spirit proceeding
> From Him: so believe
> In God and His apostles.
> Say not Trinity: desist:
> It will be better for you:
> For God is One God. (Sura IV)

Jesus was not crucified, according to Islam. Although condemned to death, his likeness was put on another man who was crucified in his place. Jesus, however, ascended to Heaven, apparently in bodily form. The second coming of Jesus provided the basis for the Islamic belief in al-Mahdi, "the guided one."

Mary and her importance are stressed in several verses in the Quran. The angel who announces to her the coming birth of Jesus says:

> O Mary! God hath chosen thee
> And purified thee—chosen thee
> Above the women of all nations....

> Behold! the angels said:
> O Mary! God giveth thee
> Glad tidings of a Word
> From Him: his name
> Will be Christ Jesus,
> The son of Mary, held in honour
> In this world and the Hereafter.... (Sura III)

A hadith states, "Every child that is born is touched by Satan and this touch makes them cry, except Maryam and her son." She is not, however, to be worshipped; she is merely "an upright woman" and, like her son, "accustomed to taking food." But Islam gives her extraordinary honors, calling her "the chief woman of Paradise."

John the Baptist, in the Quran, is called Yahya, and is regarded as a prophet. He was the first person to believe in Jesus and baptised him. Islamic legend also relates that he refused to marry the niece of Herod and was beheaded, but his head continued to speak and his blood to boil until he was exorcized by many calamities. Muslims and many other people believe that John the Baptist's head is buried in the little tomb which stands in the central courtyard of the Umayyad Mosque in Damascus.

The Quran also echoes many of the parables of the New Testament—those of the sowers, the virgins and the laborers in the eleventh hour—and the idea that the meek shall inherit the earth. Above all, Muslims believe that the Gospels foretold the coming of a new prophet, Muhammad.

During Early Islam

The bond between Muslims and Christians was strengthened when Christian Abyssinia gave asylum to Muslims when they were persecuted in Mecca. Later, however, Muhammad became critical of the Christians because of dissension between the various sects and because he believed that they had falsified their religion by worshipping not only Jesus and Mary but their monks as well.

The Christian community in Medina was not involved in the Muslims' battles with the Quraish of Mecca and faced no threat of expulsion during Muhammad's life. But after his death, the first caliph Abu Bakr, recalling the hadith "Two religions may not dwell in the Arabian Peninsula," drove them from the valley of Najran in the south, where there was a large community. Many of them must have gone over to Islam; as indigenous inhabitants they completely disappeared from the peninsula.

When the Arabs overran the largely Christian territories to the north and west of Arabia, they treated the Christians, like the Jews, as People of the Book, granting them protection and freedom to worship against the payment of certain taxes. Large numbers of Christians embraced Islam, partly no doubt through religious conviction, but also to escape taxation and to enjoy full membership in the Islamic community. The Christians who remained in the Middle East became fragmented into a bewildering number of sects. Each was allowed to administer its own communal affairs and was represented by its bishop or patriarch to the Muslim authorities. Although their social and legal status was lower than that of the Muslims, many Christians held positions of trust and power in the government and contributed much to Islamic civilization. Muslims, unlike their European contemporaries, did not insist on religious uniformity within the state.

The Crusades

Under the Islamic empire, Christian pilgrims from Europe visited the Holy Land in great numbers from the 7th to the 11th centuries.

The Emperor Charlemagne maintained diplomatic relations with Caliph Haroun al-Rashid and considered himself to be the protector of the Christians of Palestine. In 1071, however, the Seljuk Turks captured Jerusalem and dynastic wars broke out all over the Middle East. Access to the Christian holy places became difficult and dangerous, and in 1095 Pope Urban II proclaimed a crusade to rescue the Holy Land. Four years later, the Crusaders took Jerusalem by storm. Crying "God wills it" and aided by local Christians, they massacred every Muslim and Jew, man, woman and child they found in the Holy City and turned the mosques and synagogues into churches. The Norman leaders of the Crusades proceeded to turn the western seaboard of the Middle East into a patchwork of feudal states where they ruled over the Muslim populace.

At the start of the Crusades the Muslim world was in disarray and took nearly a century to find a leader capable of resisting the Christians. This was Saladin, a Kurdish general, who in 1187 recaptured Jerusalem. Unlike the Crusaders before him, he ordered that no Christian be harmed and no building looted. He released the captured knights who had families and provided from his own treasury for the widows and orphans of those killed. His prisoner, Richard Coeur de Lion, became his friend and the two signed a treaty permitting Muslim and Christian pilgrims to travel peacefully through each other's territory.

Christendom, however, continued to mount attacks against Islam. These included the Crusade of 1204, which was diverted to the sacking of Constantinople; the Children's Crusade of 1212, which enriched European slave traders; the seventh Crusade against Egypt in 1249, in which St. Louis, King of France, was captured and ransomed; and the sack of Alexandria in 1365. The chief legacy of the Crusades in the Middle East was to embitter relations between Islam and Christendom, and to disturb the relationship between Muslims and native Christians.

Under The Ottomans

The politicization of Muslim–Christian relations intensified when the Ottoman Turks gained control of most of the Arab world in the 15th and 16th centuries. They threatened Mediterranean ports, advanced into eastern Europe and were only prevented from entering western Europe by a combination of Christian armies in famous land and sea battles at Malta, Lepanto and the gates of Vienna. The hostile stance of both parties colored Christian and Muslim conceptions of each other for several centuries.

Because of their conquests, the Ottomans ruled over a large number of Christians. In most cases they treated the Christians according to the traditional Islamic code as People of the Book. They divided the religious minorities into *millets,* or "nations," allowing them to retain their own laws and customs under their own religious leaders, who were responsible to the Ottoman authorities. Turkish rule, however, was harsh and lay heavily on all citizens regardless of religion. Particularly oppressive was the Turkish institution of forced military service.

European Expansion

By the end of the 17th century the tide of power began to run in favor of Europe, and two centuries later European imperialism had engulfed most of the Muslim world. Today we see European expansion chiefly in economic and political terms, but at the time the Muslims, and to a certain extent the Christians, saw it as the triumph of one religiously defined civilization over the other. In India Britain gradually absorbed the Mughal states into its empire; and then, in order to protect the route to India, began to assume some sort of control over most of the Muslim states between Suez and the Indian Ocean. France turned to North Africa as a field of colonization, while Spain and Italy also picked up the odd pieces of territory there. The Dutch controlled Indonesia, and throughout the 19th century Russia ingested the Muslim states of central Asia. After her defeat in the First World War, Turkey was shorn of all her possessions and France and Britain awarded themselves mandates over her former Arab provinces. Between the two World Wars of this century, only a handful of Muslim states remained fully self-governing: a greatly reduced Turkey, Iran (formerly Persia), Saudi Arabia and Afghanistan.

Under Modern Islam

World War II changed all this. In the general break-up of empires, the European powers were forced to give up their hegemony over almost all of the Muslim world. Today only two major predominantly Muslim areas are controlled by non-Muslims. The larger of these is the vast southern salient of the USSR between the Caspian Sea and the borders of China. The second area that until recently was predominantly Muslim is Palestine which, under the United Nations partition plan of 1947, was divided into a Jewish and an Arab state. Israel now completely occupies all of Palestine.

9

ISLAMIC CIVILIZATION

The artistic and intellectual achievements of Islam stand as a legacy to world civilization and are a source of deep pride to every Muslim. For nearly a thousand years, beginning in Damascus in the seventh century, a remarkable creative energy flowed through the wide stretch of the Islamic world, from Spain through North Africa and the Middle East to the steppes of Central Asia and the Bay of Bengal.

Islam preserved much of the traditional culture of its founding people, the Arabs, particularly in poetry and the domestic crafts. As Islam spread, however, it absorbed other cultures with long histories of artistic and intellectual enterprise and amalgamated them with that of the Arabs. In a surprisingly short time, this synthesis produced a new civilization which was unmistakably Islamic.

As political power passed from the Arabs to other ethnic groups—Persians, Berbers, Turks, Mongols, Mughals—the original Islamic culture became the basis for further development and elaboration. The Quran and the faith provided a strong core of unity. Because of the requirement that the Quran be read and prayers recited in Arabic, the language in which it was written, Arabic became the official language throughout the early Islamic world—in law, government and education, in literature and polite discourse, as well as in religion. The Arabic alphabet became the medium of written Persian and Turkish, both of which absorbed a large number of Arabic words as well. Calligraphy was developed into a fine art with varied scripts of great beauty, some so complex in design as to be almost illegible.

Not all of those who helped create the Islamic civilization were Muslims; Jews, Christians, Zoroastrians and others contributed importantly to the artistic and intellectual development. They worked, however, within a cultural tradition initiated and guided by the Arab Muslims. During the first decade of the 8th century under the Abbasid caliphate, the first academy of thought, *dar al-hikma* ("House of Wisdom"), was founded in Baghdad. Scholars were assigned the task of researching and translating a large body of Greek knowledge—from philosophy to medicine, mathematics and astronomy. Their translation into Arabic, and later from Arabic into Latin, carried this wealth of knowledge into medieval Europe and led to the Renaissance.

But the Islamic scholars did more than translate. Building on the foundation of Greek thought, they went on to make their own outstanding scientific, literary and artistic contributions. It is not possible in this short space to give a full account of the genius of Islamic civilization. Spanning ten centuries and encompassing practically every field of human endeavor, Islam's accomplishments would fill countless volumes. Only some of the highlights can be mentioned here.

Philosophy and History

The Islamic pursuit of knowledge began with the need to define the religious tenets of the new faith and to give it a rational interpretation. Greek philosophical discipline and logic served as the guide in the Islamic desire to integrate faith and reason. The first philosopher in Islam, Al-Kindi (d.870), was an Arab and a court physician in the Abbasid caliphal court. Of encyclopedic knowledge and the author of 361 books, Al-Kindi introduced Greek philosophy into Islamic thought and tried to reconcile it with the Quran. Al-Farabi (d.925), a Turk, became important for his sociopolitical studies and is also regarded as the greatest musical theorist of his time.

Islam produced other profound and influential thinkers, many of whose works were deeply involved with Islamic theology. Among the few known in the Western world the most recognized is Al-Ghazali (d.1111). Considered the greatest theologian of Islam, he was a Persian and Sufi whose emphasis on love profoundly influenced the quality of Islamic piety. He argued against giving equal weight to reason and revelation and espoused a mystical approach to the Quran.

Three other Islamic philosophers of importance to the West were:

Ibn Sina (d.1037), a Persian known in the West as Avicenna, was a physician and a theorist of light, vision and sound. He formulated the first Islamic logic concerning the independent and interrelated existence of God, man and the universe. His medical treatises and commentaries on Aristotle were taught in medieval European universities; his works influenced Thomas Aquinas and Roger Bacon, among others.

Ibn Rushid (d.1198), also a physician, was an Arab who was born in Spain. He rejected the idea of revealed religion and advanced the theory that matter and the creative system are eternally in process of self-renewal. In this respect, he anticipated the modern theory of evolution.

Ibn Khaldoun (d.1406), a Tunisian, was the most original thinker in Islam and a pioneer in the philosophy of history and the science of sociology. His importance to the world rests on his cyclical theory of the rise and fall of civilizations, as determined by a variety of causal factors. His *muqaddima,* or preface to his *Book of Examples,* which has been translated into English and many other languages, prompted Arnold Toynbee to say, "Ibn Khaldoun has conceived and formulated a philosophy of history which is undoubtedly the greatest work of its kind that has ever yet been created by any mind in any time."

For Western civilization, Islam's greatest contribution in this field was not only the transmission, but also the preservation and interpretation of man's intellectual heritage of the past. Up until the 16th century, the works of Islamic philosophers and scientists were required study in the universities of Europe. Today, in the archives of libraries around the world lie hundreds of Arabic manuscripts still untranslated and possibly containing a store of untapped valuable knowledge from the past.

Literature

Islamic literature had its origin in the poetry of pre-Islamic Arabia. Poetry among the Arabs was considered a polished art form even then; poets were viewed as intellectuals and held in high esteem. Today, Arabs still love to hear and recite poetry and take every occasion to do so.

Long before Islam, the Bedouins of Arabia held poetry contests in which they extolled their clan and celebrated war, love and death. Poets, moreover, were the recorders of important events, oracles of the future and verbal champions of the tribe's laudatory feats. Muslims prized these poems and imitated them, even in the sophisticated circles of cities and courts.

The favorite form of poetry was the *qasida* or ode, a highly developed intricate style which follows a specific meter based on syllables. The poems are allusive in the use of personal names and the specific lore of the desert, making them difficult to translate without numerous footnotes.

Of this early poetry of the *jahiliyyah* (pre-Islamic) period, the most famous is the collection of seven odes, called the *mu'allaqat* (meaning "suspended"). According to legend, these poems had won annual prizes at fairs held in Taif and were then inscribed in golden letters and suspended on the Ka'ba wall in Mecca. Most popular of the mu'allaqat, even today, is the ode of Antar. Antar was a sixth century poet, warrior and lover whose mother was a black slave. Celebrating the early Arab ideals of valor and love, the tales of Antar's heroic deeds and his unrewarded love for his cousin Abla are legendary. In the Arab world today, to call a man "Antar" is to praise his strength and courage.

The first poets of the Islamic age rose to fame in the ninth and tenth centuries. They were Abu Nuwas, primarily a poet of erotic and sensual pleasures, and Al-Mutanabbi, who sang of the virtues of man in philosophical verse. Both were jailed during their lifetimes for heresy against the ethics and spirit of Islam, but were then released because of their poetic talents.

Another trend in Islamic poetry, which developed in Spain, resulted in verses which focused on the beauty of nature and romantic love. Famous among the poets of this school was Ibn Zaydun (d.1071), who was born in Cordova and by the age of twenty had achieved distinction for his poetry. He also spent a period in prison (for political activity), where he composed some of his greatest love poems.

Al-Muwashshah and *Al-Zajal,* two poetic forms of enduring popularity in the Arab world, also emerged in Muslim Spain. Lyric in style, these poems are often sung with music or a chorus refrain. Muwashshah, which proved to be the most radical innovation in Arabic poetry, keeps the same meter and rhyme throughout all the stanzas of the poem. Zajal, a less stylized and more popular form of verse, is credited with having given rise to the troubadours of medieval Europe.

There was also a tradition of religious verse in Islam. This originated with the mystical poets, who used profane themes of wine, intoxication and eroticism as symbols for religious ecstasy and union with God. The uninitiated may enjoy the Persian poets Sadi, Hafiz and Omar Khayyam for their sensual imagery, but this is not the only or the major import of their works. Muslim poetry still awaits a translator who can do justice to its complexity and beautiful imagery.

The Muslims also developed a prose literature alongside

poetry, but here also the language barrier and a profound difference of assumptions have prevented all but a few works from being appreciated in the West. The Quran is the supreme prose work of Islam and existing translations do little justice to the breadth and beauty of the original. The language in which it was written, Arabic, imbued as it is with the God-spoken content of the Quran, assumed an importance which structured the style and influenced the imagery of subsequent Arabic literature. Its inviolability also protected the classical unity of the language from fragmentation into dialects. (There are two forms of Arabic in use today: the classical, which is the formal language of all Arabs; and the colloquial, which varies from country to country, often drastically.)

Collections of hadiths provided the first histories of Islam and developed into the first biographies of Muhammad and his companions. These were later elaborated into more sophisticated chronicles, such as the 9th-century *Book of Conquests.* As more non-Arabs were assimilated into Islam, collections of *adab,* short pithy sayings pointing to a moral or a principle of behavior, were circulated among the people to educate them in the Arabic language, history and manners.

Secular prose was introduced with the translation into Arabic of the fables of Bidpai, a Hindu sage and writer of tales with a moral. They were originally translated from Sanskrit into Persian, but both versions were eventually lost and only the Arabic, which was translated in the eighth century, remained. Entitled *kalila wa dimna,* this collection of charming animal fables is considered a masterpiece of Arabic prose and a classic. It has been translated from

Arabic into more than forty languages and has influenced many writers, foremost among them La Fontaine.

Other prose which followed includes the *maqamah* ("discourse"), an elegant poetic style, and *alf laylah wa laylah* ("A Thousand and One Nights"), also known as *The Arabian Nights.* The creator of the maqamah was a 10th century Persian, Al-Hamadhani, who was also a well-known poet. In the 12th century the Iraqi writer, Al-Hariri, raised the maqamah to its classic form.

The Arabian Nights, like the Bidpai fables, also had a Persian source of Hindu origin. The elaboration and variety of its episodes, however, came from numerous other ethnic sources. A very popular form of literature with all classes, the tales survived and spread to Europe mostly in an oral manner. The collection was finally compiled and unified by Arab authors in the 10th century and widely translated into European languages in the 17th and 18th centuries.

Architecture

Architecture has left the most imposing monuments of Islamic civilization and the ones most accessible to us today. The Dome of the Rock in Jerusalem, the first and one of the finest examples, was built in the late seventh century by Byzantine artisans, but is unmistakably Islamic in form, decoration and function. The Umayyad Mosque in Damascus (c. 714) and the Grand Mosque of Kairouan in Tunisia (c. 862) show how Muslim architects used elements of former cultures (Roman and Greek) to construct a totally new kind of building. The Mamluk dynasty of Egypt embellished Cairo from the 13th to the 15th centuries with magnificent mosques, tombs and *madaris* (religious schools), while about the same time in Spain the Mosque of Cordova and the Alhambra Palace were built.

In 16th century Persia, Shah Abbas surrounded the main square of Isfahan with mosques, mausoleums and a pleasure palace of surpassing beauty. The Ottoman architect Sinan (d. 1556) equalled and even surpassed the great domed edifices of the Byzantines in the Blue Mosque at Istanbul and the Sultan Ahmad Mosque at Erdine. After destroying the buildings of their predecessors, the Mongols erected such splendid structures as the Tomb of Tamurlane and the Mosque of Bibi Khanoun in 15th century Samarkand. The Taj Mahal (c. 1632), a tomb commemorating the love of Shah Jahan for his wife Mumtaz-i-Mahal, is only one of the glories of Mughal architecture in India.

The Muslims rebuilt such ancient cities as Jerusalem, Aleppo, Damascus and Constantinople in more or less the form we see today. They also designed completely new cities, such as Cairo, Baghdad, the lost Madinat al-Zahra in Spain and Fathpur-Sikri in India. They installed water conduits, bath houses, fountains, drains and abattoirs long before these were common in Europe. The covered *suq* or bazaar, and the caravanserai where travelers and their pack animals lodged, were features of Muslim towns. Almshouses and hospitals, often run by charitable foundations known as *waqfs,* were well ahead of those of Europe. The Muslim city was civilized by any standards.

Visual Arts

Art in Islam functioned as an integral and intimate expression of the society. Art objects and the talents which created them were not accorded any special lofty status, but rather were considered as essential to the living environment.

Islam made little distinction between the fine arts and the applied arts, or between sacred and profane art objects. Artists deployed the same skills and styles in the making of tiles for mosques and palaces, mosque lamps and household lamps, book covers, incense burners, jewelry, armor, swords and muskets. Textiles were of special importance in Islamic life: furniture was sparse, its place taken by carpets, wall hangings and cushions; clothing was elaborate and denoted rank, profession and group status. Muslim silks, brocades and damasks were famous throughout the world ("damask" comes from Damascus, "muslin" from Mosul, a city in Iraq). Carpets from Persia, Anatolia, the Caucasus, Afghanistan and India were coveted and have been copied in the West. Small carpets, still used as prayer rugs in the Muslim world today, were often woven in silk and highly valued. Gardens, another art form, were cherished by Muslims as oases in an environment often arid, colorless and harsh.

One of the universal features of Islamic art is what the experts call aniconism, the avoidance of the depiction of solid, lifelike living creatures, especially human beings. There is no specific Quranic injunction against this, but several hadiths are invoked, especially one in which Muhammad, comparing the creativity of God with that of man, said that artists will be called upon on the Day of Judgment to provide souls for their figurative images. Aniconism was apparently an ancient Semitic tendency shared by the Jews and associated with a horror of idolatry. As a result, Islamic art is usually abstract, nonfigurative and two-dimensional. Sculpture in the round is almost totally absent.

Out of such restraint, great riches flowed. Calligraphy took the place of religious images and became an elaborate art. Muslim artists also developed a refined, sophisticated and infinitely varied repertory of repetitive, interlocking designs of two styles, one called "geometric," the other "arabesque." Artists from Spain to India created patterns in these styles and adapted them to every possible object and material, from paper to brickwork, silk to stone.

Color and overall pattern are characteristic of Islamic art, whether in carpets, ceramics or the interior or exterior of buildings. This is thought to provide visual and psychological relief from the arid landscapes that prevail in some Islamic lands, and the Muslim preference for cool blues and greens supports this theory. Architectural forms, such as the horseshoe arch, the pointed or ogival arch and the dome, were also highly developed throughout the Islamic world.

The structural requirements of mosques, law courts, shrines and other religious buildings also imposed a certain uniformity on Muslim architecture. There are local variations, as between a Moroccan and a Turkish mosque, but the essential requirements are the same.

The miniatures of Persia, Turkey and India may seem at first to contradict Islamic aniconism, with their colorful scenes of gardens, polo, hunting, battles and incidents from history and romance. For the most part, however, this was a private art hidden away in albums or as illustrations for manuscripts and available only for the pleasure of a select elite. Another example of figurative art exists in Qasr Amra, an eighth-century castle still standing well preserved in the Jordan desert, which was used by the Umayyad caliphs as a winter hideaway and hunting lodge. Its walls are covered with frescoes of dancing girls and other human figures.

Music

The sound of Islamic music of the golden age is something we must take on trust. It was not written down, but transmitted by ear, and relied on improvisation within strict conventions. Poets and philosophers praised it, artists depicted its performance and effects, and many of the instruments have survived, but the sound itself is lost to us. Orthodox Islam tended to condemn instrumental music, but encouraged the musical use of the human voice in prayer and recitation of the Quran. The word was more important than the music, a preference carried over into secular music.

As in the other arts, Islam set up a counter movement in music, independent of and even opposed to the principles of religion. Secular music was associated with luxury and pleasure and the forbidden charms of wine and public women. Concerts were typically performed by a small group of four or five instruments and the human voice. The favored instruments were drums and cymbals, flutes and reeds, bagpipes, and strings such as the lute (the word comes from the Arabic *al-Ud*), sitars and zithers. The music was strongly rhythmical and basically linear, employing much closer intervals between notes than Western music. Each player was in a sense a soloist, like modern jazz musicians, and the result was what avant garde musicians today call "aleatory," achieving accidental effects. Dancing by both men and women often accompanied music, but this again was associated with forbidden pleasures.

Education

A hadith of the Prophet recommends that the believer should go as far as China if necessary in search of knowledge, and learning has always been associated with religious concepts in Islam. The early Muslims quickly developed a complex educational system ranging from village schools to institutions of higher learning in important cities. The basis of the curriculum was the Quran, the Hadith and the Law. In grade school, studies consisted largely of learning by heart passages or even all of the Quran, as well as the rudiments of reading and writing the Arabic language. This provided understanding of grammar and also led to an appreciation of literature, including pre-Islamic poems. At more advanced stages, the students added linguistics, rhetoric, logic and other philosophical studies.

Various institutions contributed to learning. The mosque itself offered courses in the religious sciences. The *madrasa,* an independent school for boys, was often attached to a mosque or included a mosque in its premises. Boarding schools for orphans were founded, and the Fatimids in Cairo opened a boys' school to educate upper-class youths for government service. Libraries, founded by the religious authorities or by private individuals, were open to scholars. Dar al-Hikma in Baghdad contained a large library, a staff of translators, an astronomical observatory, lecture rooms and apartments for scholars. The Fatimid caliph al-Hakim later built a similar institution in Cairo, adding medicine to the curriculum.

Other Muslim rulers carried on the tradition of establishing educational foundations. Nizam al-Mulk, vizier of the Seljuk sultans, is credited with having founded the first independent boarding school for boys. Saladin, the Mamluks and Tamurlane were equally noted for their educational endowments. Although education was largely directed at males, several educated women doctors and professors are mentioned in medieval Cairo and Baghdad. In Cairo at the al-Azhar Mosque, founded in the 10th century, the idea of a university developed and was passed on across North Africa and into Spain, where it inspired the creation of the first universities in western Europe.

Science

Islam teaches that all knowledge is sacred and that all learning ultimately leads to knowledge of God. Soon after the Arabs had consolidated their early conquests, they began their search for knowledge. First the Umayyad and then the Abbasid caliphs ordered official translations of the works of classic Greek scientists and thinkers. Aristotle's *Logic* was given pride of place, with Hippocrates and Galen the chief authorities on medicine, Euclid on mathematics, and Ptolemy on astronomy. To this Greek theoretical framework and to material from Persian and Indian sources, Muslim scientists added their own original observations. Although Muslim science remained subordinated to religion, the Muslims constructed an intellectually satisfying scientific universe that was in advance of that in the West and contributed to the latter's development.

Astronomy initially became important in Islam because it helped to fix the times of prayer and the direction of the Ka'ba. The Muslims inherited a vast body of astronomical data from the Babylonians and other Middle Eastern peoples, and as desert dwellers themselves they had a natural curiosity of and reliance on the skies. As in medieval Europe, astronomy and astrology were closely linked and, despite a Quranic ban on foretelling the future, Muslim rulers had faith in horoscopes. They built elaborate observatories in Cairo, Baghdad, Damascus, Istanbul, Samarra, Samarkand and Jaipur, the remains of some of which are visible today. These observatories provided scientific data on the position of fixed stars, the movement of planets, and eclipses of the sun and moon. Many of the astronomical terms we use today, such as almanac, azimuth, zenith, nadir, and the names of stars like Aldebaran and Betelgeuse, are Arabic. Muslim astronomers constructed star maps and celestial globes and developed such instruments as the quadrant and the astrolabe for determining altitude, latitude and longitude, direction and time. Muslim astronomers also discovered contradictions in the geocentric universe of Ptolemy.

In mathematics, the Muslims created a fruitful union of Greek theory with Indian practice. Arabic numerals, so called because they came to the West through the Arabs, were invented in India, as was the concept of zero as a number (*sifr* in Arabic, from which we derive both cipher and zero). It was the Arab Muslims, however, who turned these numerals—and the vital zero—into the workable decimal system the world uses today.

Muslim mathematicians made original discoveries in the

fields of algorisms, numerical series, decimal fractions, irrational numbers, tables of tangents, geometry, trigonometry and algebra (from *al-jabr,* "bone-setting" or the reunion of broken parts). Chess, a highly scientific game, was developed by the Muslims and passed on to the West along with some of its Arabic and Persian vocabulary (i.e., checkmate, *al-shah mat,* "the king is dead").

Islamic medicine based on Greek theories, created its own system of treatment, including diet, drugs and surgery, a varied range of *materia medica,* an extensive literature on anatomy, disease and treatment, and teaching hospitals which became models for the West. Muslim physicians were familiar with the circulation of blood, the setting of broken bones, contraception, abortion, and caesarian section. Two great Muslim physicians, Avicenna and al-Razi, were considered to be the ultimate authorities in European medicine until modern times.

Muslim alchemists produced such useful substances as alum, niter, soda and iron sulphate and were able to determine the specific weight of precious stones and metals. In the field of optics, Muslims developed original theories of vision, the refraction of light and the rainbow.

Muslims were great travelers, and many of them wrote itineraries and descriptions of the countries they visited. In geography two names are pre-eminent. In the 12th century, al-Idrisi drew on various sources to produce a silver relief map of the known world for King Roger of Sicily, a Norman who employed many Muslim scholars. In the 14th century, Ibn Battuta traveled throughout the Muslim world and into India, China and Africa writing a detailed description of all that he had seen.

In technology, the Muslims invented or developed many useful devices and processes. They paid particular attention to the management of water, constructing, preserving and improving a vast network of wells and dams, irrigation canals, water wheels and windmills, cooling devices based on water and wind, and the Nilometer, a device used in Egypt to measure the Nile floods and hence predict harvests. In architecture they perfected the dome and the squinch, a device for imposing a round dome on a square base. They expended much mechanical ingenuity on making clockwork toys. In the arts of war, there were Muslim military strategists who outmaneuvered their enemies with techniques that were later adopted by European armies. Although not originally seafaring peoples, the Arabs and the Turks launched navies that commanded the local seas.

Economically, the Islamic world was nearly self-sufficient and at certain periods very prosperous. Industry and commerce benefited from the large free trade areas established within successive Islamic empires. Because of geography the Muslim world acted as middleman between the West and the Far East, carrying expensive luxury goods such as incense, silk, spices, precious metals and jewels, by ship and land caravan. In its heyday, the Muslim world imported surprisingly little from the West. By the 16th century, however, its self-sufficiency and prosperity began to decline with the dawn of the European age of discovery, world-wide trade and imperialism.

The creativity and cultural pre-eminence of Islam began to decline as well. Doubtless Ibn Khaldoun could have explained why.

10
OTHER MUSLIM BELIEFS AND PRACTICES

To an outsider the most noticeable aspects of Islam are the customs and practices that govern the everyday life of Muslims. Some of these differ from country to country, and many of them have an ethnic rather than a religious origin. As a universal system of beliefs and laws, however, Islam imposed or encouraged certain ways of behavior and forbade or discouraged others. Many of the precepts of Islam are based on the traditions of the Arabs, and naturally these traditions are strongest in the Arab countries of the Muslim world. Inasmuch as they received religious sanction, they have also affected belief and behavior in the rest of Islam.

The following are some customs and practices that at one time or another may have aroused the reader's curiosity.

The Muslim Day and Week

The Muslim clock and calendar differ from those used in the West. In recent times most Muslim countries have adopted international time systems except for religious purposes, but in some traditional countries, such as Saudi Arabia, the two systems exist side by side and are cited in official correspondence. The Muslim day begins at sunset, when clocks are reset daily to zero hour. The day is divided into twenty-four hours as in the West, an inheritance in both cases from the Babylonians. Prayer times are based on this "sun time" and strict accuracy is considered essential. Intercultural confusion can sometimes occur; for example, "Friday evening" to a Muslim means from sundown Thursday to Friday dawn, what a Westerner would call Thursday evening and night.

The Muslim week is seven days long beginning on Sunday, with the first five days named for the first five ordinal numbers: ahad (one), ithnain (two), thalatha (three), arba'a (four), khamis (five). Friday is called *jum'a,* "general assembly," as on this day every adult male is expected to attend midday prayers at the mosque. Saturday is named *sabt,* which means "sabbath."

The Muslim Year

The Muslim year is lunar, rather than solar as in the West. It contains twelve months, each beginning with the sighting of the new moon. As a lunar cycle is approximately twenty-nine and a half days long, the length of the months alternates between twenty-nine and thirty days. The lunar year is therefore 354 days long, with a leap year of 355 days about once every three years. This means that the Muslim year is from ten to eleven days shorter than the solar year, so the months move slowly forward through the seasons. Thus a given date will appear in winter, spring, summer, autumn and back to winter in a period of thirty-three years.

The Islamic era starts from the year of Muhammad's migration (*hijra*) from Mecca to Medina in 622. In the West, Islamic dates are designated Anno Hegira, A.H., on the pattern of Anno Domini, A.D. As the shorter Muslim year does not correspond exactly to that of the Gregorian calendar, a complicated formula must be used to convert the date in one system to that in the other; it is much easier to look up the equivalent date in published conversion tables. A rough guide for converting a Gregorian date to Hijra date is to subtract the figure 622 and to multiply the result by 33 over 32 (as every 33 lunar years equal approximately 32 solar years). Thus A.D. 1990 corresponds approximately to A.H. 1411.

Holidays

Two months of the Islamic year are considered especially holy: *Ramadan,* the ninth month, devoted to fasting, and *Dhu al-Hijjah,* the twelfth month, when the pilgrimage to Mecca takes place. The whole month of Ramadan is considered sacred, because it was in that period that Muhammad received the first revelation of the Quran. The last ten days of the month are especially holy, as angels are thought to descend during the night with blessings for mankind. Ramadan ends with *Id al-Fitr,* the Feast of Breaking the Fast, one of the two great Muslim holidays. The other is *Id al-Adha,* the Feast of the Sacrifice, celebrated at the end of the pilgrimage on the 10th day of Dhu al-Hijjah, when many households kill a sheep, goat or camel in memory of Ibrahim's willingness to sacrifice his son Ismail. Both of the great holidays are celebrated throughout the Muslim world with religious services, feasting and alms-giving.

A controversial holiday is *Mawlid al-Nabi,* the birthday of the Prophet, the 12th day of *Rabi' I,* the third month. Ultra-conservative Muslims like the Wahhabis frown on the celebration of any human being as a derogation from the single-minded worship of the One God. But in other societies, Muslims celebrate the Prophet's birthday with great joy and pomp. The Shi'ites also celebrate the birthdays of Ali, Fatima, Hasan and Husain. New Year's Day, the first of *Muharram,* is a holiday in most Muslim countries, though not all.

The 27th of *Rajab,* the seventh month, is the anniversary of the Prophet's miraculous Nocturnal Journey and ascension to Heaven; pious Muslims spend the night in mosques reading stories of the ascension. The night of 14th *Sha'ban,* the eighth month, is devoted to prayers for the dead and to visiting and cleaning the tombs of the departed. On the 10th day of *Muharram* Shi'ite Muslims mourn the death of Husain. They go on pilgrimage to his tomb in Karbala and perform a passion play about his death.

The Mosque

The word mosque has its roots in the Arabic *masjid,* meaning "place of prostration." Used primarily as the place of communal prayer, the mosque also serves as a forum for important proclamations of interest to the community. In early Islam, the mosque was the center of society and often served as a court of justice.

The basic requirements of the mosque are few and

simple. They consist of a prayer hall large enough to accommodate the congregation. The floor of the hall is covered with carpets or mats. In one wall is set the *mihrab,* a niche indicating the direction of prayer towards Mecca. Next to this is the *minbar,* a flight of steps leading to a small platform from which the *imam* (prayer leader) or other prominent Muslims stand to deliver addresses, usually religious in character but sometimes political as well. All mosques of any size and consequence have a minaret (sometimes more than one) from which the call to prayer, now usually recorded, is issued. Most mosques also have washing facilities outside the prayer hall where worshippers perform the necessary ablutions before prayer.

Around these essentials mosque architecture has evolved in many different styles. Some are simple and austere without decoration. Others are elaborate structures of domes, columns, courtyards and *diwans* (recessed walls), decorated with marble, colored tiles, mosaics, carvings and gilding, and furnished with fine carpets, crystal chandeliers and richly decorated *kursi Quran* (book rests for the Holy Quran). Some mosques contain the tombs of renowned Muslims, and many have libraries, hospitals and schools attached to them.

Mosques are usually endowed with income-producing property by their founder or their ruler; today in Muslim countries they are supported by the state or by an administrative organization called the *waqf.* There are several kinds of mosque officials to ensure efficient functioning of the mosque. The *nazir* or *wali* controls finances and has overall jurisdiction. The *imam* leads prayers and often delivers sermons. The *muezzin* calls the faithful to prayer. Other officials clean, maintain and guard the mosque.

The mosque is always open for meditation, study and private prayer. There are no priestly intermediaries or organized ecclesiastical authorities in Islamic religion; man's relationship with God is a direct, private communion. The nearest approach to clergy in Islam are the *ulama* (from *ilm,* "knowledge"), who are theologians and jurists; and anyone with faith and a knowledge of the Quran can become a religious leader. As individuals or in schools, the ulama may interpret the Quran and the Sunna, but they have no authority to change or modify orthodox dogma in any way.

Dietary Laws

The dietary laws of Islam resemble those of the Jews but are much less strict. The Quran declares:

> Forbidden to you are: dead meat, blood,
> The flesh of swine, and that on which hath
>   been invoked
> The name of other than God;
> That which hath been killed by strangling,
> Or by a violent blow, or by a headlong fall,
> Or by being gored to death;
> That which hath been partly eaten by a
>   wild animal;
> Unless you are able to slaughter it in due form;
> That which is sacrificed on stone altars.
>   (Sura V)

The pig is the only animal that is specifically forbidden, the other prohibitions having to do with methods of death and with pagan sacrifice. Tradition, however, has classified other animals as unclean and therefore forbidden: beasts and birds of prey, crawling things, dogs, and those animals which men are specifically forbidden to kill (the hoopoe, for example, because this bird with a handsome fanlike crest carried messages for Solomon). The fitness of other animals for food was debated by the law schools. All agreed that the ass and the mule were forbidden, the camel and the ox allowed; some permitted horseflesh, others forbade it; one school permitted foxes, hyenas and elephants; locusts and lizards were allowed. One school permits all that live in or on water, the other three only fish. Game is clean if the hunter pronounces the name of God when he shoots or sets his hounds on the prey.

No animal is lawfully edible unless it has been properly slaughtered. The correct procedure is for the butcher to turn the animal's face towards the Ka'ba, pronounce the name of God, cut the animal's throat and allow the blood to drain from the body. Even game that has been shot or brought down by a hunting hound should have its throat cut in the prescribed way. Fish need not be killed, the mere catching of it being sufficient. The meat of animals butchered by Jews and Christians is lawful but it is better not to eat it.

Alcohol

The ban on the consumption of alcohol sets Islam apart from the rest of the world. At the beginning of his mission, Muhammad's followers were permitted to drink intoxicating beverages, but the Prophet's revelations of God's word led gradually to a prohibition of them. This progression is seen in verses of the Quran. An early verse says, "And of the fruit of palm trees and grapes you obtain an inebriating liquor, and also good nourishment." A little later, "They will ask you concerning wine and gambling. Answer, in both there is great sin and also some things of use to men, but their sinfulness is greater than their use." It was not until drunkenness had interfered with prayer that the ban was made absolute: "O true believers, surely wine and gambling . . . are an abomination, the works of Satan. Therefore avoid them that you may prosper." The ban is reinforced by several hadiths, i.e.: "Cursed is he who drinks, buys, sells wine or causes others to drink it." The law schools extended the prohibition to distilled spirits when they became available in the Muslim world.

Although the ban is categorical, the attitudes of Muslim societies throughout history have been equivocal about the drinking of wine. The Sufis used intoxicants in their mystic rites, and Muslim poets have sung of the delights of wine. In Paradise, according to the Quran, "Their thirst will be slaked with pure wine." A few Muslim countries today, notably those under Wahhabi influence, prohibit the manufacture, import, sale and possession of alcoholic beverages and punish severely those who disobey the law.

Hospitality

Hospitality to friends and strangers alike is an important tradition in Muslim society, with roots reaching back to the Bedouin culture of the Arabian desert, where distances were great and food and water scarce. Wayfarers approaching a Bedouin encampment with peaceful intentions were fed and housed for a limited time (usually three days).

Even an enemy could, under elaborate conventions, expect to be received safely for a limited period. Much of the spirit of this age-old hospitality continues to the present day. It is seen in the custom of serving refreshment—coffee, tea, fruit juice or the like—as soon as a guest arrives, whether in a tent, a home or a business office.

Good table manners are more than a tradition among the Muslims; they are sanctioned by the example and sayings of the Prophet as described in many hadiths. The name of God should be pronounced at the beginning and end of every meal. The food should be taken in the right hand only, the left being reserved for unclean things. The hands should, of course, be washed at the beginning and end of the meal.

Dogs

 The Muslim attitude towards dogs is somewhat ambivalent. According to several hadiths, it is an unclean animal. The presence of a dog makes prayers worthless and renders a room impure for ritual purposes. The Arabic word for dog, *kalb,* is used as a term of abuse. On the other hand, working dogs, whether used for hunting, guarding or herding, are acceptable; and the saluki, the greyhound of the desert from Morocco to Iran, is held in high esteem and trained to course after hare and gazelles.

Circumcision

Circumcision of males, a custom shared with the Jews and now routine in many Western countries, has always been practiced in Islam. It is not, however, prescribed in the

Quran, perhaps because it was so universal among the Arabs that it needed no comment. Pre-Islamic poetry mentioned it, and tradition states that the Prophet was born circumcised as a mark of divine favor. The age of circumcision varies geographically from the seventh day after birth to the thirteenth year, and the occasion is celebrated with festivities. Whatever its religious connotations, circumcision is part of the Muslims' concern for personal hygiene. The ritual washing five times a day before prayer reflects this concern.

Women

In Islam, women are spiritually equal to men and share in all the religious duties and rewards of Islam. Standards of personal status, such as marriage, divorce and inheritance, may differ from those of the West; Quranic law and tradition, however, confer on women many protective rights.

Historically, female rights always and everywhere have been to some degree inferior to those of the male. In Arabia before Islam, unwanted baby girls were allegedly exposed to death; men could take as many wives as they pleased; and husbands took possession of their wives' property and held it even after divorce. Muhammad greatly improved the lot of women. Under Islamic law, all children, male or female, are to be equally cared for and protected; polygamy, though retained, is limited to four legal wives and is placed under other restrictions; married women retain control of their property during marriage and after divorce; widows and divorced wives have status and are protected.

Under Islam women have long had certain rights—especially those pertaining to property and inheritance—which women in Europe and the United States did not gain until recently.

Muhammad had high regard for women. He married often and had concubines as well. But women were more than sexual objects in his life and in the early history of Islam. Khadija, his first wife, was his earliest convert and his greatest support when he was alone and unhonored. His young wife Aisha was the support of his old age and a doughty fighter in the wars of succession following his death. She had a profound effect on the development of Islam both as a political force and as the source of a large number of hadiths. Through his daughter Fatima (and her husband Ali), the whole line of Shi'ite caliphs claimed descent from the Prophet and the divine right of succession. Others among his wives, daughters, female relatives and supporters are venerated among the earliest examplars of Islam.

The religious equality of men and women is affirmed in both the Quran and the Hadith. This is shown by the fact that the Quran often employs both masculine and feminine nouns and pronouns. Women are specifically enjoined to perform the five duties or Pillars of Islam. One sura reads: "Men who surrender to Allah and women who surrender, and men who believe and women who believe, and men who speak the truth and women who speak the truth, and men who persevere in righteousness and women who persevere, and men who are humble and women who are humble, and men who give alms and women who give alms, and men who fast and women who fast, and men who guard their modesty and women who guard their modesty, and men who remember Allah and women who remember—Allah has prepared for them forgiveness and a vast reward." A hadith quotes the Prophet as saying: "All people are equal as the teeth of a comb. There is no claim of merit of an Arab over a non-Arab, or of a white over a black, or of a male over a female. Only God-fearing people will merit a preference with God."

The face veil for women and the segregation of the sexes are not enjoined in the Quran. Most women in pre-Islamic Arabia did not wear the face veil, and from certain stories it is clear that the faces of many female followers of Muhammad were visible. Even today, women do not wear the veil when on pilgrimage to Mecca. Veiling appears to have been a Byzantine and Persian custom which was introduced among the Arabs in the ninth century and became a status symbol. Even in traditional Arab societies today, veiling is largely an urban and middle class practice. Peasant and Bedouin women do not cover their faces, though they may do so at the approach of a stranger. In many Islamic countries, the custom of veiling has been dying out and some states have made it illegal. However, a counter-current encouraged by Islamic revivalism is appearing. In Iran under the ayatollahs, the *chador,* a long robe that covers the head but not the face, has been reimposed on women; in some other Muslim countries, women are readopting the Islamic *hijab* (veiling) as a reaction to secularism and Westernization.

Segregation of the sexes was the custom of pre-Islamic

Arabia and so seemed natural to Muhammad and his companions. This was probably a protection for women in a harsh and sometimes lawless society. Today the degree of segregation in Islam varies from country to country. Within the family, segregation traditionally takes the form of the *harim.* Harim simply means "forbidden" and denotes the women's rooms in a house, which are forbidden to strangers; it does not imply confinement. A typical harim contains the wife or wives (and in the old days, concubines), all small children of both sexes, unmarried female relatives and female servants. In conservative Muslim societies, segregation is also imposed in public places such as schools, mosques, restaurants, and beaches. Segregation is not imposed during the pilgrimage.

Polygamy. The unrestricted polygamy of pre-Islamic Arabia was reduced in the Quran to four legal wives with the injunction that the husband treat all of them equally. "Marry the women who seem good to you, two or three or four, but if you fear that you cannot do justice to them one only... thus it is more likely that you will not do injustice." The Quran then advises: " You will not be able to deal equally between your wives however much you may wish to do so." The message clearly is that, while polygamy is permitted, monogamy is preferable. Today polygamy is outlawed in some states and is dying out naturally in others.

The marriage contract. Marriage in Islam is a contract between the two parties containing terms mutually agreed upon. Although many marriages are arranged, the consent of both the bride and groom must be freely given.

The man pays a dowry according to his circumstances, and also specifies the amount of alimony to be paid in event of divorce. What wealth the woman may bring to the marriage remains her property. In traditional societies a Muslim wife keeps her maiden name. Although traditional Islam makes a wife subservient to her husband, many Muslim couples can be as happy and loving as those in other cultures, a fact confirmed by Muslim history and literature as well as by personal observation. Beneath the obvious patriarchal tradition, there is in practice a strong presence of matriarchal power in Muslim families. The final word in all matters relating to the family belongs to the father but is often exercised by the mother.

Divorce. As for divorce, classical Islam gave the man a great advantage over the woman. The Quran enshrined the old Arab tradition of allowing the man to repudiate his wife simply by pronouncing *talaq* (the formula of divorce) three times. Again, Muhammad tried to redress an inequality. To prevent the impulsive declaration of talaq, reasons for the proposed divorce must be stated, an interval is required between each pronouncement, and most jurists require that talaq be pronounced before a qadi, who is bound to try to reconcile the parties. The Quran also introduced a period of waiting in case of pregnancy. If divorced, the wife retains the dowry, her own property, and is paid the alimony promised her. A man may not remarry a divorced wife until she has been married and divorced by another man. A strong inhibition to divorce is the hadith in which Muhammad said, "Among things permitted, talaq is the most hated by Allah."

The wife also has the right to initiate divorce. This is called *faskh* and is more limited than talaq. The wife must have valid reasons for dissolving the marriage; these include insanity, undue cruelty, impotence, nonpayment of the dowry, nonsupport, change of religion, noncompatibility, or nonfulfillment of other obligations under the marriage contract.

Many Islamic states have abolished talaq and made divorce laws more equitable, either by extending Quranic principles by means of analogy or by adopting Western laws alongside the Shari'a.

Inheritance. Islamic laws strictly define inheritance. Wives and daughters usually inherit half as much as the sons, and if there are no sons the daughters may have to share the estate with other male relatives. This is based on the tradition that men are required to provide for women in their care, while women are under no such obligation.

Muslim women are subject to other legal inequalities. In law courts the testimony of two women is required to equal the testimony of one man. In the most traditional countries, women do not drive automobiles or ride alone in taxis. Women may also be required to obtain the permission of their husband or other male guardian in order to obtain a passport to travel abroad.

Education. Most Islamic countries provide equal opportunities for education of women. Schools are sometimes segregated below university level. Today, in the modernizing Muslim countries, females attend classes at every level, and have entered many professions traditionally the domain of men.

Historical records frequently mention individual women who reached a high level of learning. Female doctors and professors practiced and taught in medieval Baghdad and Cairo. In the 19th century women were attending law classes in the courtyard of the Holy Mosque at Mecca.

Although their proper sphere is considered to be the home and family, Muslim women since Khadija, Fatima and Aisha have often wielded considerably wider influence. Zubaida, the wife of a caliph of Baghdad, is still remembered for her benefactions to pilgrims (including a road across the Arabian peninsula that bears her name), and the sister of Saladin, Sitt al-Sham ("The Lady of Syria") was noted for her educational foundations. The tombs of female Marabouts are venerated throughout North Africa. In Muslim India women rose to political power. In 1236, Radiya, daughter of the sultan of Delhi, was appointed over the heads of her brothers and ruled the state for four years. The great Mughal, Akbar, was under the influence of his wet-nurse and gave his wives control over the imperial seal, without which decrees and appointments were not valid. For a time during the 17th and 18th centuries, the so-called Reign of Women flourished in Istanbul. A series of ruthless and intelligent women, many of European descent, ruled the Ottoman court as *Valide Sultana,* "the mother of the sultan," obtaining through intrigue the succession of their sons, dismissing and appointing ministers, launching wars and directing foreign relations through the confines of the imperial harim. In Lebanon in the 20th century strong matriarchs have been an effective force in feudal groups in that country.

Such women are exceptional in any society. But the fact

that they exist in Islam shows that the religion and culture have not stifled female initiative. The Muslim woman has some way to go before she achieves equality with men, but it is a mistake to think that she is without rights and influence.

Slavery

Slavery, though recognized in the Quran and in the Law (as it was in both the Old and New Testaments), is today illegal throughout Islam. As members of the United Nations, all Muslim states have accepted the obligation under the UN Charter (carried over from the League of Nations protocol of 1926) to abolish chattel slavery in their domains. In some states, where slavery was abolished only recently, former slaves continue to work for their masters as free employees. Vestiges of slave systems may remain in some remote areas of countries where there is little government control.

Islamic slavery, however, was an extremely interesting institution, differing in many ways from its counterpart in the West. Although the possession of slaves was permitted by religion and society, slaves were protected by Quranic injunctions, the Hadith and the Law from extreme exploitation by their masters. As in the case of marriage and women's rights, the tendency of Muhammad's teachings was to ameliorate an inherited situation. Another of the striking characteristics of Islamic slavery was that slaves were often socially, politically and economically superior to free men and that slave origins were no bar to advancement to the highest office.

The Quran exhorts believers to be kind to slaves. A hadith said that anyone who beats a slave could be forgiven only if he set the slave free. Manumission of a slave was a meritorious act rewarded in heaven, and most Muslim slaves eventually obtained their freedom. Some of them bought themselves out; the master was expected to set a low price in such cases and to help financially; a portion of the zakah, or alms-tax, was set aside for this purpose. The freed slave of a Muslim master remained a client of his former owner and received his patronage and protection.

A man was not permitted to marry his own slaves, but if a concubine bore a child to her owner, she became *umm walad,* "mother of the child," and her status changed. Henceforth she could not be sold or otherwise alienated, and on the death of her master she was set free. The children of an umm walad by her master were born free and the Law made no distinction between the children of a free mother and those of a slave. Some caliphs had slave mothers; the Ottoman sultans never married free women and were all the sons of concubines.

One of the most curious aspects of Islamic slavery was the corps of **Mamluks,** a word meaning owned or possessed which was applied to a white military slave. When the Ottomans first spread into the Middle East, many of their soldiers were Mamluks. Because of their aggressiveness, bravery and military skills, they became stronger and more numerous, seized power from their masters and came to rule in some areas. In Egypt in the 13th century, Mamluks purchased by the Ayyubid dynasty revolted and created their own dynasty; though technically slaves, they ruled over the free populace and possessed much of the wealth of the nation. Slave soldiers also came to power in India. A handful of Europeans, captured and turned into slaves, also rose to eminence. A Scot, Thomas Keith of Edinburgh, was captured at the Battle of Rosetta and became the slave of a Muslim prince, who appointed him governor of Medina in 1817. A Dutch cabin boy taken by slavers from the American sailing ship *Salem* became the favorite of the ruler of Oman and inherited his position. European women captured by Barbary pirates became the mothers of amirs and sultans.

Prayer Beads and Amulets

Prayer beads (*subha* or *misbaha*) are a common sight in the Islamic world, carried by Muslims and non-Muslims alike. They are made of various substances—coral, amber, bone, glass, ivory, silver, agate, pearl or sweet-smelling wood. A misbaha consists of thirty-three beads (or multiples thereof) divided into groups of eleven which are separated by a single differently shaped bead, the whole terminated by a long bead called a *yad* (hand). The beads are used to count the 99 beautiful names of God (The Exalted, The Generous, The Creator, The Compassionate...), or to count off a series of prayers. Sometimes they are simply fingered as a distraction, hence the popular name "worry beads." The musbaha is not considered to be holy in itself, and Muslims frequently present them as gifts to non-Muslim friends.

Talismans or amulets are widely used throughout the Islamic world to bring good luck or to ward off the evil eye. They usually consist of a short verse of the Quran or one of the 99 names of God inscribed on a stone, shell or metal, often encased in gold or silver and worn on the person. A popular form of talisman is the human hand, imprinted on the walls of a house or fashioned in metal and worn as an amulet. It is called the Hand of Fatima, and the five fingers represent Muhammad, Ali, Fatima, Hasan and Husain. These have no religious significance.

Religious Expressions

The speech of Muslims is filled with religious words and phrases to an extent not known in the modern Christian world. Muslims have a formula for almost every social and human occasion, often with a sort of echoing reply. To name only four of these, the most widely used: The salutation *salaam* means "peace" or "health" or "well-being." It is used in various forms, the most common being *as-salaam alaikum,* "peace be upon you," to which the reply is *wa'alaikum as-salaam,* "and upon you peace." Another phrase in constant use is *bi ism Allah* (pronounced bismalla) and meaning "in the name of God." It is pronounced at the beginning of every important endeavor, at the beginning and end of meals, and written on almost everything from documents to buildings. The phrase *insh' Allah,* "if God wills," is pronounced by Muslims whenever the future is referred to, indicating that only God knows the future. Finally, *al-hamdu lillah,* "praise be to God," is said after the mention of any successful venture.

Weddings and Births

Muslim wedding customs differ from place to place and reflect local traditions, as indicated by the fact that

Muslims and Christians living in the same locality have similar traditions. The festivities, usually segregated by sex and lasting three days, include singing and dancing, the serving of sweets and drinks, but no alcohol, and among the Bedouin the killing of one or more sheep to be eaten by the guests. In North Africa, the Bedouin stage a mock kidnapping, perhaps in memory of a time when brides were literally captured. In other circles the bride is accompanied by her female relatives and friends when she goes to meet the groom.

Customs marking the birth of a child also differ from place to place and class to class. One widespread custom is to whisper into the right ear of a newborn child the words of the *adhan,* the call of the muezzin announcing the time of prayer:

> *God is most great.*
> *I testify there is no god but Allah.*
> *I testify that Muhammad is the apostle of Allah.*
> *Come to prayer.*
> *Come to salvation.*
> *God is most great.*
> *There is no god but Allah.*

GLOSSARY

The following alphabetical list contains the words and proper names which appear frequently in any discussion of Islam.

Abbasid. Arab dynasty founded in 762 which reigned as caliphs of Sunni Islam in Baghdad until overthrown in the Mongol invasion of 1258.

Abd. Slave or servitor, either in the legal sense or in the religious sense of the individual's relationship to God. It forms part of such proper names as Abd Allah ("Slave of God") and Abd al-Karim ("Slave of the Most Generous").

Abu. Father, used in such proper names as Abu Bakr and Abu Talib.

Ahl al-kitab. "People of the Book," principally Jews and Christians, so-called because they possess written scriptures in contrast to the heathens. They were therefore protected and allowed to worship freely on payment of a poll tax.

Amir (also spelled ameer, emir, etc.). Commander, used as both a military and civil title and in such compounds as *amir al-bahr* (admiral) and *amir al-hajj* (leader of a pilgrim caravan).

Ansar. "Helpers," the title given to Muhammad's first converts in Medina and later to all those who helped in his campaigns.

Ashab. "Companions," the title given to Muhammad's earliest converts in Mecca who accompanied him to Medina.

Ashariya. "Twelvers," a sect of Shi'ite Islam recognizing twelve Imams or leaders. They form the majority in Iran and a large minority in Iraq.

Ayyubid. Dynasty founded by Saladin (Salah al-Din al-Ayyubi) in the 12th century and which ruled Egypt, Syria and Palestine for two centuries.

Bairam. Turkish word for festival or holiday, used in Turkey and Egypt and other countries once under Ottoman influence.

Bedouin (also spelled Badawin). Dweller in the desert; a nomad.

Berber. Natives of North Africa originally speaking a Hamitic tongue but now almost complete Arabized. They ruled parts of Spain from 1086 to 1248.

Bid'a. "Innovation," the opposite of *sunna* or tradition and hence considered wrong or heretical.

Dar al-harb. "Abode of war," those countries not subjected to Islam.

Dar al-Islam. "The abode of Islam," a country under Muslim rule.

Dhimma. "Covenant"; People of the Covenant are non-Muslims in a Muslim country who are guaranteed rights to life, liberty and property.

Diya. Blood money; compensation paid under the law for injury or homicide.

Faskh. Right of the wife to initiate divorce.

Fatiha. Opening chapter of the Quran frequently recited in prayer.

Fatwa. Legal opinion of a mufti or canon lawyer.

Fikh. "Intelligence," "understanding" ; the term used for jurisprudence in Islam. Fikh books are collections of legal decisions creating precedents.

Hajj. Pilgrimage, especially the pilgrimage to Mecca, one of the five pillars of Islam. A pilgrim is a *hajji* (fem. *hajjia*)

Halal. That which is legally permitted, as opposed to *haram,* forbidden.

Hanafi. School of law practiced in Turkey, Western Asia, India and Lower Egypt.

Hanbali. School of law predominant in Saudi Arabia.

Hanif. Follower of an innate form of monotheism, neither Jewish nor Christian, which existed in Arabia prior to Islam.

Haram. Sacred or forbidden, applied (often in the dual form of haramain) to the two holy cities of Mecca and Medina and in the singular to the sacred enclosure surrounding the Dome of the Rock in Jerusalem.

Harim. Part of a house forbidden to strangers, in which the women of the household reside.

Hijra (spelled Hegira in English). Emigration, denoting Muhammad's flight from Mecca to Medina in 622. This marks the beginning of the Muslim era, the dates of which are designated Anno Hegira, A.H.

Ibn. Son, used in such proper names as Ibn Sa'ud.

Id. Festival; the two great religious festivals of Islam are *'Id al-Adha,* the Feast of the Sacrifice, and *'Id al-Fitr,* the Feast of Breaking the Fast.

Ihram (from haram, forbidden or sacred). The white seamless garment worn by pilgrims making the pilgrimage to Mecca.

Ijma'. Agreement or consensus. In practice this is the consensus of the learned members of the community only, one of the sources of Islamic law after the Quran and the Sunna.

Imam. Leader, especially the leader of a group in prayer. In Shi'ite Islam imam is used to mean the caliph or leader of the entire body of the faithful.

Isa. Muslim name for Jesus, considered to be an Islamic prophet.

Ismaili (from the proper name Ismail or Ishmael). Member of one of the major sects of Shi'a Islam.

Jahannam. Muslim name for Hell.

Jahiliyyah. Name given to the state of things in Arabia before Islam, translated as the Age of Ignorance.

Janna. "Garden," Paradise or Heaven in the Quran.

Jibril (Gabriel). One of the four archangels, the angel of Revelation, who brought the Quran to Muhammad.

Jihad. Holy war against unbelievers; it can also mean a peaceful crusade.

Jinn. Invisible creatures made of fire; like mankind, capable of salvation or damnation.

Kharijite. "Seceder," member of a sect of Sunni Islam which emphasizes the need for purity in true believers.

Khitan. Circumcision, a requirement for all male Muslims.

Madrasa. School where the Islamic sciences are taught; any school for students up to age 17 or 18.

Mahdi. Guided one, a messianic figure who will appear at the end of time to rule the world in justice and righteousness.

Malak (plural, malaika). Angel, the servant and messenger of God.

Maliki. School of Law predominant in Upper Egypt, North and West Africa.

Mamluk (also spelled Mameluke). Slave. Historically mamluk came to mean a white slave as opposed to *abd,* a black slave. A caste of military slaves called Mamluks ruled in Egypt and Syria from the 13th to the 15th century.

Marabout. Local saint or his descendant in North Africa; also the tomb or shrine of such a saint.

Masihi. Christian, from al-Masih, the Messiah.

Mawali. Originally freed slaves, later non-Arab converts to Islam.

Mihrab. Shallow niche in a mosque indicating the *kibla,* or direction of prayer towards the Ka'ba in Mecca.

Millet. Nation; the Ottoman Turks divided society into autonomous religious groups known as *millets,* each governed by a bishop or rabbi.

Minaret. Tower beside or attached to a mosque from which the call to prayer is made.

Minbar. Pulpit, a set of steps in mosques from which preachers deliver sermons.

Mosque. Muslim place of worship.

Mozarab. Arabized; in Spain the term was applied to Christians and Jews who converted to Islam.

Muezzin. One who calls the faithful to prayer.

Mufti. Canon lawyer or jurisconsult of higher standing than a *qadi.*

Mughal. Variation of "Mongol," designating the Turkish-Mongol conquerors of India who ruled parts of the subcontinent from the 15th to the 19th century.

Mut'a. Form of temporary marriage for a fixed period on payment to the woman, recognized by some Shi'ite sects but not by Sunnis.

Nabi. Prophet, a term applied to Biblical prophets as well as to Muhammad.

Nasrani. One from Nazareth, a Christian.

Nusairi. Member of an extreme Shi'ite sect from northern Syria.

Ottoman (from Osman, the Turkish version of Uthman, a proper name). Turkish dynasty that conquered Constantinople in 1453 and founded an empire lasting till the end of the First World War.

Qadi (sometimes spelled cadi or kadi). Judge in a religious court.

Qanum. Regulations independent of Shari'a Law.

Qarmatians. A sect from eastern Arabia who conquered a large part of the Arabian peninsula in the 10th century.

Qibla. Direction of the Ka'ba in Mecca, towards which Muslims face in prayer.

Qiyas. Analogy, a method by which Muslim courts extend the principals of Islam to cover parallel cases.

Ramadan. Ninth month of the Islamic year, when Muhammad received the first revelation of the Quran; Muslims are required to fast from dawn till sunset during Ramadan.

Rasul. Messenger or apostle, the title given to Muhammad in the Muslim testimony of faith.

Sab'iya. "Seveners," Shi'ite sect that recognizes seven Imams.

Sadaqa. Voluntary alms, as opposed to *zakat,* the alms-tax.

Safavid. Shi'ite dynasty that came to power in Iran in the mid-15th century and ruled till the end of the 17th. They made Shi'a Islam the state religion.

Salah. Ritual prayer, divine service, one of the five pillars of Islam.

Sawm. Fasting; one of the five pillars of Islam.

Seljuks. Turkish tribe that ruled over large parts of the Middle East in the 11th century.

Shafi'i. School of Law practiced in Syria, Lower Egypt, India and Indonesia.

Shahada. Testimony in both the legal and religious sense; one of the five pillars of Islam.

Shaikh. "Elder," a title of respect.

Shaitan. Satan, the Devil.

Shari'a. "The path to the watering place," the whole of Islamic law comprising the Quran, the Sunna, *ijma'* (consensus) and *qiyas* (analogy).

Sharif. Noble of high descent; used especially for the descendants of Muhammad through Ali and Fatima.

Shirk. Association of another with God; polytheism.

Sufi. Member of a mystical religious order.

Sultan. Turkish military title, assumed by the head of the Seljuk and Ottoman Turks and in other parts of the Islamic world.

Sura. Chapter of the Quran.

Talaq. Form of divorce in which the husband repudiates his wife by pronouncing "talaq" three times.

Ulama. Body of learned men in an Islamic community qualified to pronounce consensus on matters relating to religion and social usage.

Umayyads. First hereditary Arab dynasty of Sunni Caliphs (661-

750) who ruled in Damascus when the Arab empire was at its height.

Umm al-walad. Concubine who has given birth to her master's child thus entitling her to certain privileges.

Umra. Minor pilgrimage, a visit to Mecca and the Ka'ba at any time of the year outside the time of the major Hajj.

Wahhabi. Member of an Islamic sect or community in Saudi Arabia that believes in a return to the way of life of early Islam.

Waqf. Official foundation for the administration of mosques and state charities.

Zaidi. Member of a moderate Shi'ite sect prevalent in Yemen.

Zakat. Alms-tax, one of the five Pillars of Islam.

Zamzam. Holy well in the courtyard of the mosque at Mecca from which all pilgrims drink.

SUGGESTIONS FOR FURTHER READING

Religion

Abdallah Yousef Ali: THE GLORIOUS KUR'AN (Lahore 1934, 1st edition), Abd Al-Rahman 'Azzam: THE ETERNAL MESSAGE OF MUHAMMAD (New York 1962), and Mohammed Marmaduke Pickthal: THE MEANING OF THE GLORIOUS KORAN: AN EXPLANATORY TRANSLATION (New York 1976) describe the faith of Islam from the point of view of the devout believer. Fazlur Rahman: ISLAM (Chicago 1979) offers an authoritative description and interpretation of Islam. Alfred Guillaume: IS-LAM (London 1981) gives a sympathetic account of Islam from the Christian point of view. Kenneth Cragg: THE CALL OF THE MINARET (Maryknoll, NY 1986) and THE ARAB CHRISTIAN: A HISTORY IN THE MIDDLE EAST (Louisville, KY 1991) is an Anglican bishop, poet, Islamic scholar, and sensitive interpreter of the Quran. John L. Esposito: ISLAM: THE STRAIGHT PATH (New York and Oxford 1992) is a comprehensive, sound and detailed account. Mohammad Jawad Chirri: THE PROPHET'S BROTHER (Detroit 1978) presents the Shi'ite position as to succession after Muhammad. Akbar S. Ahmed: LIVING ISLAM: FROM SAMARKAND TO STORNAWAY (New York 1994) describes, with lively prose and color photos, Islam as practiced today; based on BBC TV series.

History

Carleton S. Coon: CARAVAN: THE STORY OF THE MIDDLE EAST (Huntington, NY 1976) places Islam in the context of Middle Eastern history. THE CAMBRIDGE HISTORY OF ISLAM (Cambridge 1977) is an authoritative account of the history of Islam as a religion and a political movement. Bernard Lewis: THE ARABS IN HISTORY (London 1966 and New York 1967) and Peter Mansfield: THE ARAB WORLD: A COMPREHENSIVE HISTORY (New York 1976) recount the role of the Arabs in the genesis and growth of Islam, as does Michael Rogers: THE

SPREAD OF ISLAM (Oxford and New York 1976). H. W. Hazard: ATLAS OF ISLAMIC HISTORY (Princeton 1952) and William C. Brice, Editor: AN HISTORICAL ATLAS OF ISLAM (Leiden 1982) present the history of Islam in maps and diagrams of great clarity. Albert Hourani: A HISTORY OF THE ARAB PEOPLES (Cambridge, MA 1991) is acclaimed for its scholarship, literary grace, and balance. Francis Robinson: CAMBRIDGE ILLUSTRATED HISTORY OF THE ISLAMIC WORLD (New York 1996) stresses interaction between Islam and the West.

Civilization

Wilfred Blunt: THE SPLENDOURS OF ISLAM (London and New York 1976), Titus Burckhardt: ART OF ISLAM: LANGUAGE AND MEANING (London 1976), and Bernard Lewis, Editor: THE WORLD OF ISLAM: FAITH, PEOPLE, CULTURE (London 1977) survey Islamic civilization in words and pictures. Joseph Schacht and C. E. Bosworth, Editors: THE LEGACY OF ISLAM (Oxford 1974) evaluates Islam's contributions to world culture. Philip K. Hitti: ISLAM: A WAY OF LIFE (Chicago 1970) examines Islam not only as a religion but also as a state and culture. Ahman Y. al-Hassan and Donald R. Hill: ISLAMIC TECHNOLOGY: AN ILLUSTRATED HISTORY (Cambridge and Paris 1986) present several challenging theses, one of them that Islamic technology continued to flourish to the end of the 17th century. Halim Barakat: THE ARAB WORLD: SOCIETY, CULTURE AND STATE (Berkeley, CA 1993) provides a major text for teachers and students of Middle Eastern civilization. M. M. Badawi: A SHORT HISTORY OF MODERN ARABIC LITERATURE (Oxford UK 1993). A concise survey of Arabic literature since the mid-19th century by a well-known historian and critic; useful bibliography.

Present-day Islam

Edward Mortimer: FAITH AND POWER: THE POLITICS OF IS-LAM (New York 1982 and London 1983) studies the words and actions of Muslim political leaders throughout history and in selected countries today. G. H. Jansen: MILITANT ISLAM (London 1979) describes the ferment in Muslim communities across the globe. Michael Gilsenan: RECOGNIZING ISLAM (London 1983) examines the internalization of Islamic principles in secular societies today. Fatima Mernissi: BEYOND THE VEIL: MALE-FEMALE DYNAMICS IN MODERN MUSLIM SOCIETY (Bloomington, IN 1992) is a revised edition of an authoritative study of women in Islam. Elizabeth Warnock Fernea: CHILDREN IN THE MUSLIM MIDDLE EAST (Austin 1995) presents attitudes and ongoing research relevant to global concerns about children. Sayyed Hosein Nasr: TRADITIONAL ISLAM IN THE MODERN WORLD (London 1987), Akbar S. Ahmed: DISCOVERING IS-LAM: MAKING SENSE OF MUSLIM HISTORY AND SOCIETY (London and New York 1988), and Ahmed's LIVING ISLAM: FROM SAMARKAND TO STORNAWAY (New York 1994) all offer stimulating insight into the condition of modern Islamic society.